CONFLICT IN THE 20TH

SOUTH AND CENTRAL AMERICA

Dr JOHN PIMLOTT

FRANKLIN WATTS

London · New York · Toronto · Sydney

INTRODUCTION

South and Central America together constitute one of the least understood regions of the modern world. To many outsiders, its countries seem to be politically unstable, economically weak and prone to violence. To the United States, the area is one of potential (or actual) crisis; to the Soviet Union, it seems to be ripe for left-wing political change, which would increase communist standing in the world.

These views all contain an element of truth. Although the majority of South and Central American countries received their independence from Iberian (Spanish and Portuguese) colonial rule as long ago as the 1820s, few have avoided deep internal divisions leading to revolutions, *coups d'état* and civil wars. Social problems, particularly between the "haves" and "have nots" in societies with extremes of wealth and poverty, have for long fuelled internal violence. In such circumstances, the growth of left-wing ideologies has been unavoidable, thrusting the region into the maelstrom of the more general East-West divide.

It is the East-West problem which has caused the most dangerous crises since 1945. The United States, ever aware of the political, strategic and economic importance of its own "backyard", has consistently intervened to ensure pro-Western governments stay in power. This has taken a variety of forms, ranging from economic aid to all-out military invasion. Few of the crises have been completely resolved, however, taking on more global significance as Soviet and Cuban influence has increased.

But it would be wrong to presume that the picture is entirely bleak. Some South and Central American countries have managed to develop both politically and economically, avoiding the endless round of violence and exploiting their abundant natural resources. Indeed, by the mid-1980s, a definite trend towards democracy – rule by an elected government – was apparent. Violence will undoubtedly continue and crises recur, but an increased awareness by outside countries of the region's unique problems provides the key to the future.

Dr John Pimlott *Series Editor*

EDITORIAL PANEL

Series Editor:
Dr John Pimlott, Senior Lecturer in the Department of War Studies and International Affairs, RMA Sandhurst

Editorial Advisory Panel:
Brigadier General James L Collins Jr, US Army Chief of Military History 1970-82

General Sir John Hackett, former Commander-in-Chief of the British Army of the Rhine and Principal of King's College, London

Ian Hogg, retired Master Gunner of the Artillery, British Army, and editor of *Jane's Infantry Weapons*

John Keegan, former Senior Lecturer in the Department of War Studies and International Affairs, RMA Sandhurst, now Defence Correspondent, *Daily Telegraph*

Professor Laurence Martin, Vice-Chancellor of the University of Newcastle-upon-Tyne

A Nicaraguan National Guard armoured car advances through deserted streets in 1978. Nicaragua was subject to a guerrilla campaign mounted by the Sandinistas during the 1970s. In 1979 the unpopular Anastasio Somoza (Junior) fled the country and the Sandinistas were able to seize power.

CONTENTS

Chapter 1	**A Troubled Continent**	6	
Chapter 2	**From World War to Cold War**	16	
Chapter 3	**Guerrillas**	26	
Chapter 4	**Ideological Arena**	36	

Appendices
Personalities 48
War and Revolution since 1900 50
Major Guerrilla Groups 52
Debt 54
The Drugs Connection 56
Chronology 58

Index 60

Acknowledgements 62

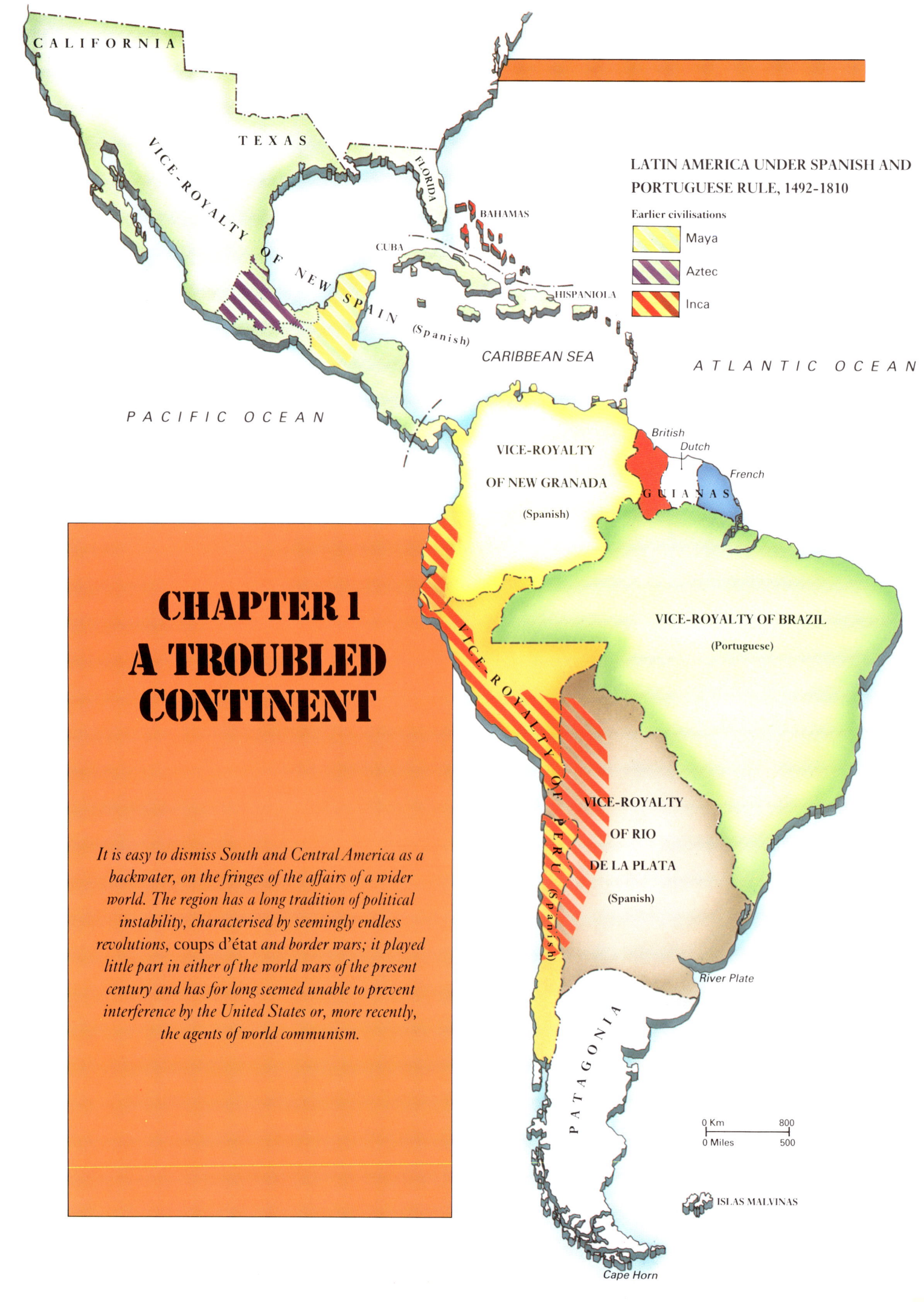

CHAPTER 1
A TROUBLED CONTINENT

It is easy to dismiss South and Central America as a backwater, on the fringes of the affairs of a wider world. The region has a long tradition of political instability, characterised by seemingly endless revolutions, coups d'état and border wars; it played little part in either of the world wars of the present century and has for long seemed unable to prevent interference by the United States or, more recently, the agents of world communism.

LATIN AMERICA UNDER SPANISH AND PORTUGUESE RULE, 1492–1810

Earlier civilisations
- Maya
- Aztec
- Inca

A TROUBLED CONTINENT

With ever-growing international debts – in 1987 estimated at $360 billion – and a population of more than 400 million, many of whom are doomed to lives of grinding poverty, South and Central (Latin) America would appear to have little to offer its own people, let alone the rest of the world.

But this is a gross generalisation, ignoring the region's history and its potential. Although problems undoubtedly exist, it is both short-sighted and dangerous to use them as a basis for dismissing the region from the mainstream of world affairs. South and Central America constitutes a storehouse of natural resources and, as the development of superpower rivalry in the area implies, it occupies a geo-strategic position of major importance, not least in terms of the Panama Canal and Cape Horn.

Moreover, despite the political, social and economic pressures, some countries within the region have made sustained efforts to solve their problems, achieving a degree of power and influence which cannot be ignored. In such circumstances, it is important to understand the region and its history, avoiding the generalisations it is often so tempting to make.

The discovery of America

The first "Americans" came from northeast Asia, crossing the Ice-Age landbridge to Alaska in about 15,000 BC. Gradually more sophisticated societies emerged – the Maya and Toltecs in Central America, the Aztecs in Mexico and the Incas in Peru. The latter were at their height when, at the end of the 15th century AD, the first Europeans arrived.

On 12 October 1492, Christopher Columbus landed in the Bahamas convinced that he had reached the spice islands of Asia by a new, western route. He went on to discover Hispaniola (present-day Haiti and the Dominican Republic) and Cuba, before returning to Spain in triumph.

A second expedition the following year established the first European settlement and, amid reports of gold and silver just waiting to be picked up, a substantial influx of Europeans began.

Using the Caribbean islands as bases, so-called *conquistadores* moved to Panama in 1513. In 1520 Hernán Cortés smashed the Aztec empire in Mexico at the head of a force of only 600 men, and some 12 years later Francisco Pizarro did the same to the Incas in Peru and Chile.

Part of a huge coffee plantation in Brazil. Coffee is a major export commodity in Central and South America.

The Portuguese took over Brazil. It was a remarkable achievement, spurred on by the discovery of vast silver deposits in Peru and Mexico in the 1540s.

The empires

The Iberian (Spanish and Portuguese) empires in America lasted until the beginning of the 19th century, by which time the flow of precious metals had begun to decline. Even so, as late as 1800 Spanish America alone was still providing nine-tenths of the world's gold and silver. The decline prompted other European powers to encroach on Spanish-held areas, hoping to grab a share of the wealth.

By 1800, Britain held Jamaica and a host of smaller Caribbean islands, as well as settlements on the mainland in Belize (British Honduras) and Guyana (British Guiana). Both the French (in French Guiana and the Caribbean) and the Dutch (in Surinam) had also muscled in. But their holdings were tiny compared to the vastness of the Spanish and Portuguese possessions, divided into the vice-royalties of New Spain (from California to Panama, including the Caribbean), New Granada (Venezuela, Colombia and Ecuador), Peru (Peru and Chile), La Plata (Argentina, Bolivia, Paraguay and Uruguay) and Brazil.

Imperial rule

But tensions were already apparent which were to lead to the independence of these areas and the creation of modern Latin America. For much of the imperial period, Spain and Portugal had maintained close control over their American possessions, ruling them with an iron hand through specially appointed governors who ensured that the flow of precious metals continued. The fact that these governors were invariably Iberian-born led to growing resentment among the European settlers (known collectively as *creoles*). They felt quite naturally that they had a much clearer idea of the needs of their region.

Goods required by the new towns and cities of Latin America could only be bought from the government, and trade with Britain, France and, after 1783, the United States was not permitted. Landowners were subject to taxation from Madrid or Lisbon, yet were not permitted to develop their land as they saw fit. What emerged was a highly centralised, bureaucratic form of government which many *creoles* quickly learned to undermine. In this, they were joined by *mestizos* (people of European and Indian blood) who resented their low status in colonial society.

Reforms

As so often happens, the drive towards independence was preceded by reform of the old system. Thus, under the rule of Carlos III and Carlos IV, between 1759 and the 1790s, Spanish America was gradually opened up to wider trade and local politics were broadened to include selected *creoles*.

At much the same time, the Marquis of Pombal, chief minister to Joseph I of Portugal, introduced similar reforms in Brazil, and when this coincided with new liberal ideas flowing from the American and French Revolutions, demands for independence grew.

The result was a dramatic and far-reaching revolution in the affairs of Latin America. Spain and Portugal, weakened by French invasion, rapidly lost their grip and, between 1810 and 1822, were forced to accept the reality of colonial loss.

In many cases, independence came through the actions of powerful leaders such as Simon Bolívar and José de San Martin, establishing a tradition of personal influence which is still apparent today; elsewhere, the move to independence was more reluctant, leading to "invasions" by liberating forces and a blurring of territorial boundaries between the new states.

Simon Bolívar, 1783-1830.

A TROUBLED CONTINENT

SOUTH AND CENTRAL AMERICAN INDEPENDENCE FROM 1804

- Central American Confederation 1821-38
- Federation of Gran Colombia 1820-30
- British possessions
- Dutch possessions
- French possessions

Bolívar the Liberator

Thus, for example, the military actions of Bolívar in New Granada were initially countered by Spanish troops in 1811-12, after which he was forced to rebuild his forces in the Orinoco estuary. Meanwhile, in La Plata the local *creoles* had seized power for themselves, opening up Buenos Aires to free trade in 1810, but they too were defeated by Spanish troops in Upper Peru (renamed Bolivia in 1825) as well as by fellow *creoles*, wary of domination by Buenos Aires, in Paraguay.

In Chile, it took the strategic genius of San Martin to gain control (in 1818), but he was forced to impose independence on neighbouring Peru, which tried to remain loyal to the Spanish crown. Elsewhere, the independence of Mexico owed as much to Spanish-born activists as it did to resentful *creoles*. Brazil took a different, but no less dramatic, course in 1822, declaring itself independent under the rule of King Pedro I, son of the Portuguese monarch.

Independence

The effects of independence varied, although it is safe to say that the broad mass of the people – those who did not own land and enjoyed few, if any, political rights – probably noticed little difference in their everyday lives. Power was transferred from one set of whites to another, leaving the Indians, *mestizos* and African slaves to carry on much as before.

Soon the dreams of a Latin American confederation fell apart under the growing pressures of regional differences and nationalism. Individual countries began to clash. This, in turn, opened the way for interference by outside powers.

Internal unrest

These three themes – domestic inequality leading to unrest, territorial disputes and foreign intervention – coloured the development of most Latin American countries throughout the 19th and early 20th centuries. Immediately after independence, for example, the social divisions within many of the new countries produced clashes which were soon to develop into revolutions, military *coups d'état* (the takeover of political power by armed force) and civil wars, some of which were to last for years. The divisions took a variety of forms.

First, and most obvious, the struggle between the *creoles* and the lower, non-white classes, for land, wealth and power inevitably led to bitter resentment. In El Salvador, for example, the so-called "fourteen families" owned virtually all the land, treating the peasant population (almost 90 per cent of which was *mestizo*) as little more than slave labour. Although in this particular case, it was to take until 1930 for a "peasant revolt" to break out, internal unrest was a constant feature for almost a century, weakening the country by draining its resources and preventing economic development. It was a pattern repeated throughout the continent.

Conservative-liberal splits

Another split was that between *creoles* who could not agree about the form of government to be adopted in the new countries. Those who followed "conservative" beliefs strongly supported the Catholic Church (often a major landowner in its own right), pursued the ideal of strong central government and stood firm against the introduction of new political ideas.

They were opposed by the "liberals", who believed in the principles of freedom put forward by the American and French Revolutions of the late 18th century, distrusted the power of the Church and dedicated themselves to undermining the influence of the ruling families. As this particular split was apparent in Guatemala, Nicaragua, Venezuela, Ecuador, Peru and Paraguay at various times throughout the post-independence period, it inevitably constituted a major factor in the history of Latin America as a whole.

Urban and rural splits

There was more to it than this, however, for quite often the conservative-liberal split acted as a disguise for more fundamental differences about the way individual countries should be run. In some cases, the people living in the remote rural areas of the interior favoured a much freer system of government than those who lived in the cities or on the coast. The latter, enjoying the benefits of wealth and trade, wished to retain and develop their power, and so favoured a strong, centralised government: they were known as "centralists". Their opponents, wishing to retain the freedom associated with "frontier" life, called for a looser form of rule, with each region looking after its own affairs and owing no more than a nominal allegiance to the central government: they were known as "federalists" or "regionalists".

In Argentina, this split led to conflict between Buenos Aires (the centralists) and the *gauchos* (cowboys) of the grasslands of the interior (the regionalists) which plunged the country into chaos until 1861, when Buenos Aires finally came out on top.

Caudillos

In such circumstances, settled government, based on the principles of democracy, was impossible to create and, in many cases, it was the strongest who ended up in control. As their strength invariably came from access to weapons, a tradition of *caudillos* (powerful

Emiliano Zapata, peasant leader in Mexico.

Mexicans killed by US troops, Vera Cruz, 1914.

men) backed by armies which ranged from organised national forces to little more than bandit gangs, became firmly fixed. Honduras, for example, suffered 134 *coups d'état* in 134 years after the break-up of the Central American Confederation in 1838.

The rise of the middle classes

But it would be wrong to presume that every Latin American country dissolved into instant chaos the moment it achieved independence. Costa Rica, for example, settled down to enjoy ordered government as early as 1838. Quite often it was the emergence of middle classes (professional people such as doctors, lawyers and teachers, allied to traders and small farmers) that broke the deadlock, demanding a share in government which was denied to them so long as *caudillo* rule continued.

The Mexican Revolution

Occasionally, however, the deadlock persisted despite changes in the make-up of society, and in these cases it was left to the lower classes – the landless peasants – to organise revolution to achieve a more equal distribution of power. The results were bloody, producing civil war as the dictators clung to the privileges they enjoyed, and nowhere was this more true than in Mexico at the beginning of the 20th century.

After years of war, foreign intervention, civil unrest and border disputes, Mexico achieved a measure of stability in 1876, when Porfirio Díaz seized power in a military-backed *coup d'état*. He managed to impose order by armed force and the country began slowly to recover. However, Mexican mineral resources were sold to foreign investors or speculators, landowners were encouraged to expand their estates by taking over Indian land and, by 1910, an estimated three-quarters of the population of 20 million were living in abject poverty. Revolution became inevitable.

It began in 1910 when Francisco Madero, a liberal-minded landowner, led a protest against Díaz's autocratic rule. Almost immediately, he was joined by a charismatic peasant leader, Emiliano Zapata and, despite the overthrow of Díaz, a civil war ensued. Madero was murdered by an ambitious general in 1913, who in turn was defeated by a combination of forces under Venustiano Carranza, and another peasant leader, Pancho Villa.

The fighting did not end until 1920, by which time Zapata and Carranza were dead, the country had been "invaded" by a military force from the United States, and a soldier, Alvaro Obregón, had emerged as president. He managed to restore order and, between 1920 and 1924, to introduce social reforms which defused the peasant anger.

Economic progress

Such events, in Mexico and elsewhere, took place against a backcloth of economic development which, in some cases, was quite dramatic. When the Iberian rulers had departed in the 1820s, most of Latin America had been barely self-sufficient, depending almost entirely upon underdeveloped agriculture for its survival and upon foreign imports for more sophisticated needs. This began to change in the late 19th century, when a variety of countries discovered valuable mineral resources such as copper, tin and nitrates, or started to exploit their one great advantage of seemingly limitless land.

Wealth began to flow, attracting foreign investment (which fuelled economic growth) and, more importantly from a social point of view, large-scale immigration, particularly from the poverty-stricken areas of Europe. Population figures increased dramatically – in Argentina, for example, the number of citizens was put at eight million in 1914, four times that of 1870 – and this triggered the development of land hitherto ignored. Railways were built to connect new towns and villages – a total of 24,000 km (15,000 miles) of track in Brazil alone by 1914 – new industries were introduced and foreign trade established. In some cases, the "boom years" did not last long, cut short by the "Great Depression" of the early 1930s, when global economic problems led to a decline in trade.

Border disputes

The emergence of so many separate countries in Latin America made border disputes inevitable, for once the idea of confederation had collapsed in the 1830s, with both Gran Colombia and the Central American Confederation splitting up, the process of establishing precise territorial boundaries began. Where the geographical area was small or already developed, this led to clashes between emerging governments almost immediately: indeed, in Central America a tradition of cross-border interference, sometimes amounting to all-out invasion, was soon established.

Guatemala, for example, gained a reputation for such action, particularly during the presidency of Rafael Carrera (1838-65), who used his superior armed forces to attack El Salvador and Honduras on a number of occasions, most notably 1839, 1850 and 1863. His successor, General Justo Rufino Barrios, continued the trend, being killed at the head of his army as it advanced yet again into El Salvador in 1885.

A similar pattern emerged on the island of Hispaniola, where Haitian troops overran the Dominican Republic in 1822, ruling the area for 22 years in the so-called "Period of Africanisation". Haitian policies were so repressive that the Dominicans remained fearful of their neighbour for years, even persuading Spain to "re-annex" (resume control of) their country for a couple of years in the 1860s before turning for more effective support to the United States.

Further south, where vast areas of Latin America had yet to be explored, this type of interference was less common, although this did not prevent border clashes. In 1825, for example, Argentina and Brazil fought for control of the area to the north of the River Plate estuary and, despite the creation of Uruguay as a buffer between them three years later, this remained a cause for war as late as the 1850s.

Similar border clashes occurred between Argentina and Bolivia (1837-39), while Peru managed to fight Colombia (1827), Chile (1838), Bolivia (1841) and Ecuador (1859) in its efforts to carve out acceptable boundaries. Very occasionally, the enemy was non-American – in 1866, for example, Peru, Chile, Ecuador and Colombia sank their differences to oppose Spanish attempts to dominate the trade routes of the eastern Pacific – but the vast majority of clashes remained purely Latin American affairs, hidden from the scrutiny of outside powers and contributing to the growing reputation of the continent as a region of instability.

19th century wars

Nor was this entirely unjustified, for some of the clashes developed into full-blown wars, leading to substantial losses in terms of manpower and, for the defeated countries, border territory. In 1865, Paraguay tried to interfere in the internal politics of Uruguay, supporting the "centralists" in the long-running battle for control in that country, only to find that this alienated both Argentina and Brazil, united in their backing for the "regionalists".

In the so-called Triple Alliance War (1865-70) Brazil, Argentina and Uruguay joined forces to defeat and occupy Paraguay, only withdrawing after substantial tracts of border land had been transferred to their control. Nine years later, on the other side of the continent, Chile went to war with Bolivia and Peru over the right to exploit newly discovered minerals in remote provinces claimed by all three countries. The War of the Pacific went on until 1883, resulting in a Chilean victory and occupation of the disputed ground, cutting Bolivia off from access to the sea.

A TROUBLED CONTINENT

One of the results of Latin American independence in the 1820s was the creation of border disputes between the new countries. Some of these developed into regional wars – notably between Bolivia and Paraguay (1932-35) and between Peru and Ecuador (1941) – while others produced tensions which threatened the stability of Latin America as a whole.

SOUTH AND CENTRAL AMERICAN BORDER DISPUTES, 1899 TO THE PRESENT

- to Brazil from Venezuela 1904-05
- PANAMA gained independence from Colombia 1903
- to Brazil from French Guiana 1900
- to Brazil from Colombia 1904-05
- to Colombia from Ecuador 1922
- to Peru from Ecuador 1942
- to Brazil from Bolivia 1902, 1909
- to Brazil from Bolivia 1927
- to Peru from Chile 1929
- Chaco ceded to Paraguay from Bolivia 1938
- disputed by Argentina and Chile 1899-1902
- FALKLAND ISLANDS claimed by Argentina
- Beagle Channel disputed by Chile and Argentina

The Chaco War

The desire to regain such access became a central feature of Bolivian policy and led to further fighting, this time against Paraguay, in the early 1930s. Denied direct outlets on the Pacific coast, Bolivian rulers began to explore the possibility of access to the Atlantic down the Paraguay river as it flowed through the Paraguayan province of Chaco. Border clashes occurred in 1927-28, leading to full-scale conflict in 1932.

The Chaco War continued until June 1935, by which time both sides had suffered enormous casualties. Paraguay gained overall military victory, along with 52,000 sq km (20,000 square miles) of disputed territory, although the Bolivians were allowed rail access to the river. At the same time, a similar war was being fought between Peru and Colombia over a small strip of territory on the upper Amazon known as Leticia.

The fighting, which lasted from 1932 until September 1935, was never as bitter as that in the Chaco area, but it did lead to domestic problems in both countries and resentments over the costs of the war. Despite an eventual settlement of the dispute in favour of Colombia, Peru was not deterred from further border clashes: in 1941 Peruvian forces invaded Ecuador, occupying the provinces of El Oro and Oriente in a war which involved tanks, artillery, airpower and naval forces. The tradition of local wars had clearly become well established, as had foreign intervention.

Mexico

As early as the 1820s, for example, citizens of the United States began to settle in the Mexican province of Texas and, in 1836, they declared their independence, defeating a Mexican army under the command of Antonio López de Santa Anna.

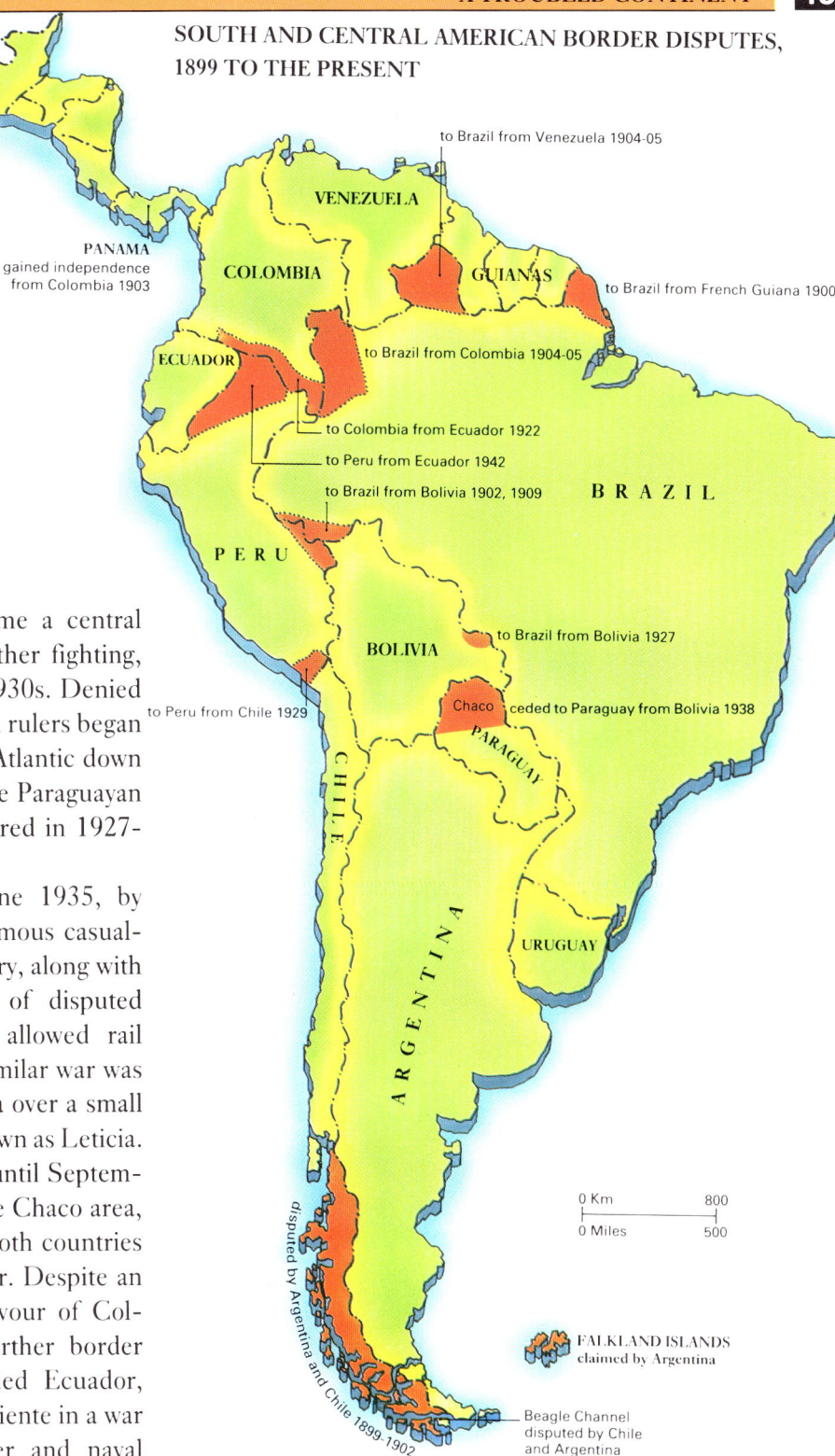

Invasion

This was followed by an invasion of Mexico by the United States in 1846, a year after Texas had joined the Union, and by the end of the war, Mexico was forced to give up New Mexico, California, Utah, Arizona and part of Colorado. Nor was this the only example of outside interference. In 1862 the French were angry at Mexico's failure to honour debts.

CONFLICT IN THE 20TH CENTURY

They intervened not only to force repayment but also to install Archduke Maximilian of Austria as Emperor of Mexico. The plan backfired when the United States chose to support the previous president, Benito Juarez; he was able to mobilise the people and defeat French troops sent to protect the new emperor. By 1867 Maximilian was dead and the republic had been restored.

US intervention

The United States had always been concerned about the security of Latin America. As early as 1823 the Monroe Doctrine (named after President James Monroe) had stated that the United States would actively oppose any further European attempts to colonise the Americas, and this became a central feature of US foreign policy.

It was shown most forcibly over Cuba, which had remained a Spanish possession despite the events of the 1820s elsewhere. Aware of Cuba's strategic importance, only 145 km (90 miles) from Florida and dominating the trade routes of the Caribbean, US presidents had tried on a number of occasions to purchase the island from Spain, but with no success. Thus, when the Cuban people rose against their colonial masters in 1895, implying that the Spanish hold was weak, it was only natural that the situation should be watched by the United States.

Three years later, in February 1898, the battleship USS *Maine* blew up in mysterious circumstances in Havana harbour, and this was taken as a cause for war. The campaign lasted only three months, but at the end of that time Spain had been forced not only to relinquish Cuba but also to hand over to the United States the colonies of Puerto Rico (in the Caribbean), Guam and the Philippines (in the Pacific). In 1901, the Platt Amendment laid down that US troops would be stationed in Cuba until the right of the United States to intervene "for the preservation of good government" had been enshrined in the Cuban constitution, and although the troops were withdrawn in 1933, the US still retained the naval base at Guantanamo.

The Panama Canal

This policy of active intervention was followed throughout Central America and the Caribbean, triggered to a large extent by plans for the construction of a canal to link the Atlantic and Pacific oceans. In 1903, the United States tried to persuade Colombia to allow the canal to be cut through the province of Panama, where the isthmus is particularly narrow, and when the Colombian government hesitated, especially over US demands for full control of territory surrounding the waterway, influential landowners in Panama were persuaded to declare the independence of their province under US protection.

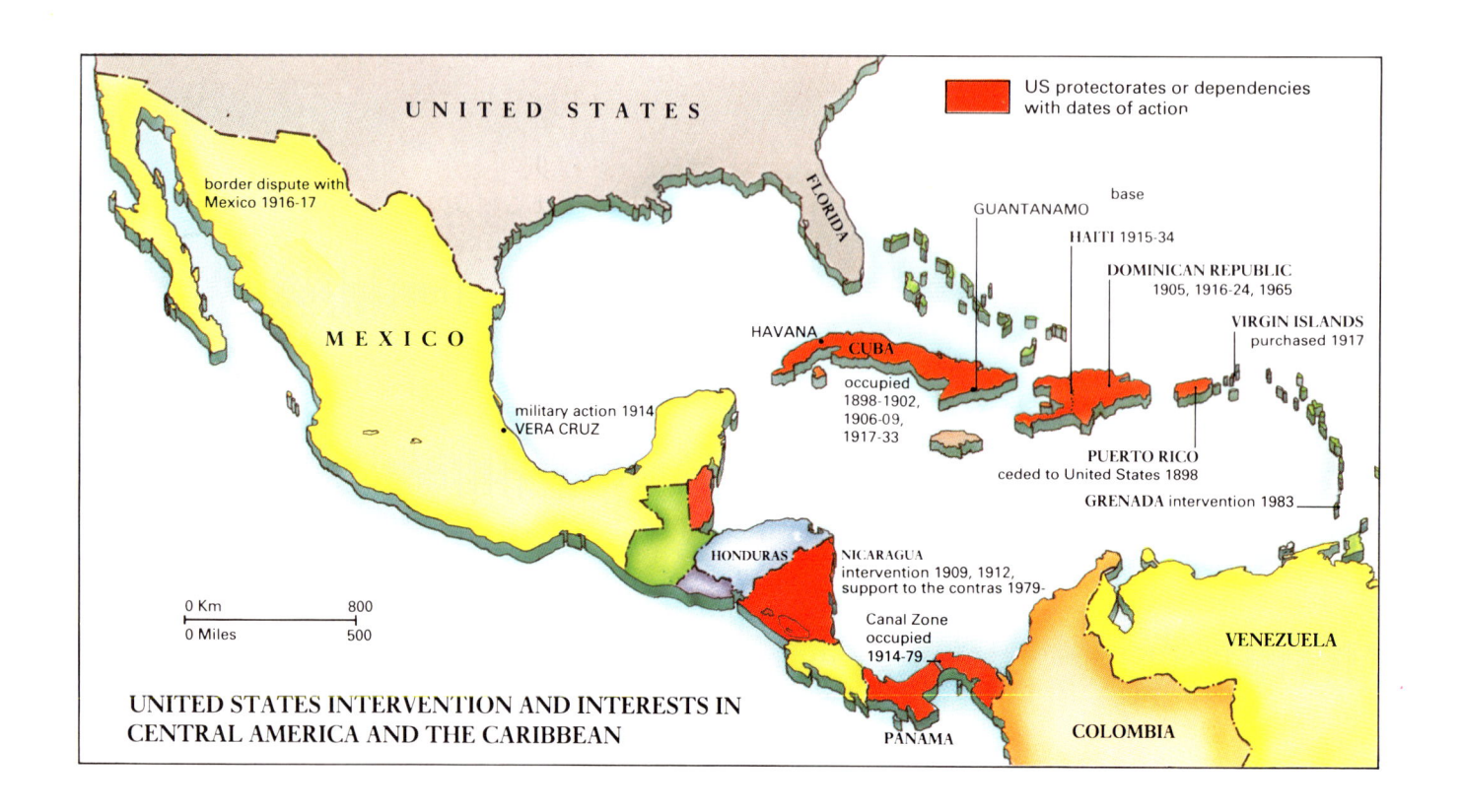

UNITED STATES INTERVENTION AND INTERESTS IN CENTRAL AMERICA AND THE CARIBBEAN

US protectorates or dependencies with dates of action

- border dispute with Mexico 1916-17
- military action 1914, VERA CRUZ
- GUANTANAMO base
- HAITI 1915-34
- DOMINICAN REPUBLIC 1905, 1916-24, 1965
- VIRGIN ISLANDS purchased 1917
- CUBA occupied 1898-1902, 1906-09, 1917-33
- PUERTO RICO ceded to United States 1898
- GRENADA intervention 1983
- NICARAGUA intervention 1909, 1912, support to the contras 1979-
- Canal Zone occupied 1914-79

A US ship in the Panama Canal – a vital strategic waterway.

US control

Colombia, powerless to respond, consequently lost a significant tract of territory, a new Latin American country emerged and, when the Panama Canal finally opened in August 1914, the United States gained full control of a strip of land on either bank, designed to ensure "free passage" for all US ships in the future.

By then, President Theodore Roosevelt had asserted the right of his country to intervene anywhere in Latin America to maintain "good government" (the Roosevelt Corollary to the Monroe Doctrine), a policy which led to intervention in the Dominican Republic (1905), Nicaragua (1909), Haiti (1915) and Mexico (1916-17). At the same time, US money was poured into selected countries, partly to shore up friendly governments but also to make them dependent on their northern neighbour. The idea was that in the event of crisis, these governments would be forced to act as Washington dictated for fear of losing economic aid, which was essential to their survival.

The Good Neighbour scheme

But this was extremely expensive and, as the United States reeled from the shock of the Great Depression in the early 1930s, the policy had to be modified. In January 1933 the newly elected President Franklin D Roosevelt introduced a more subtle approach, based on the theme of friendly co-operation rather than direct force. His "Good Neighbour" scheme implied a more equal relationship between the United States and Latin America, and when this was coupled to a Reciprocal Trade Agreements Act in 1934, in which the United States promised special trading privileges to selected Latin American countries, the era of active intervention seemed to be over. But this could not disguise the fact that the United States had become fully aware of the strategic, political and economic impact of Latin American affairs and was willing, directly or indirectly, to influence them to suit her needs. It was a trend that was to be developed considerably further both during and after the Second World War.

Admiral Graf Spee, scuttled in 1939.

CHAPTER 2
FROM WORLD WAR TO COLD WAR

The Second World War (1939-45) had a number of effects upon the countries of Latin America. Very little actual fighting occurred in the region and only a few countries actively participated in campaigns elsewhere. However, the Allied demands for raw materials led to an economic "boom" and, more significantly in the long term, regional co-operation, under the leadership of the United States, began to emerge.

By 1945, Latin America was finding a common voice in world affairs, made stronger by the virtual disappearance of European influence, except in the small number of surviving colonies.

The Second World War

When war broke out in Europe in September 1939, the American republics (the United States and independent Latin American countries together) remained aloof, determined not to be drawn in. As early as 23 September, their foreign ministers met in Panama and declared the Americas to be a neutral area, with a 480 km (300 mile) security zone around the coast, within which all warlike acts would be forbidden.

Three months later, British cruisers encountered the German battleship *Admiral Graf Spee* in the South Atlantic and, after an action well within the security zone, forced their damaged enemy to seek shelter in Montevideo harbour. The Uruguayans insisted that the *Graf Spee* should leave after only a short time and, rather than face a superior British force offshore, the German captain chose to scuttle (deliberately sink) his ship as it cleared the River Plate estuary.

No Latin Americans were involved in the battle and the Uruguayans had stuck firmly to the rules of neutrality, but it was obvious that none of the belligerents was prepared to recognise the security zone. Subsequent submarine activity by the Germans in the Caribbean and close to the Atlantic coast of the Americas merely reinforced the point.

Relations with Europe
Even so, none of the American republics declared war on the Axis powers (Germany, Italy and Japan) until after the United States had been drawn into the conflict by the Japanese attack on Pearl Harbor (7 December 1941). Indeed, the United States began to have an increasing influence in foreign affairs. In July 1940, for example, in the immediate aftermath of the German occupation of France and the Netherlands, it was the United States which called another foreign ministers' conference, this time in Havana (Cuba), to co-ordinate the policy of the republics. In this case, the Roosevelt Corollary to the Monroe Doctrine was reasserted. It was agreed that if and when European colonies in the Americas were in danger of falling under foreign (non-American) control, the republics would step in and take over their administration.

Pro-German feeling
It was not easy to achieve Latin American co-ordination, however, as the United States discovered when it tried to persuade the republics to create a solid front against the Axis powers. During the 1930s a number of countries had been attracted by the fascist ideas of strong government control, tied to the appeal of nationalism, and they were reluctant to declare war on Germany, Italy or Japan, even after Pearl Harbor.

Thus, when Washington called another meeting of American representatives at Rio de Janeiro (Brazil) in January 1942, the idea of a regional declaration of war was opposed by Argentina (which was notably pro-Axis) and Chile (which feared for the security of its long Pacific coastline). The United States had to be content with a recommendation that the republics should sever diplomatic and trading links with the enemy, but some countries did decide to go further.

In fact, by May 1942 all the Central American and Caribbean republics had declared war on the Axis and, three months later, Brazil followed suit, having suffered as a result of Germany's decision to attack neutral shipping carrying cargoes to Britain or the United States.

Active involvement
In the event, Mexico and Brazil were the only Latin American countries to take an active part in the war. In 1943 a Brazilian Expeditionary Force was sent to Italy, seeing hard fighting as part of the Allied advance to Rome and beyond, and in 1945 Mexico contributed a squadron of fighter aircraft to the closing stages of the Pacific campaign.

By then, Axis defeat was inevitable and the United States was able to renew its demands for greater involvement. It was also announced that no one who had remained aloof from the war would be invited to the San Francisco Conference to set up the United Nations (UN).

Bolivia and Ecuador had already joined the Allied camp and, in February 1945, as the republics met again, at Chapultepec (Mexico), others did the same. By April, on the eve of the San Francisco Conference six more countries – Paraguay, Chile, Peru, Venezuela, Uruguay and even Argentina – had declared war, helping to form a solid bloc of Latin American influence in the UN.

The Organisation of American States
The Chapultepec meeting was equally important in terms of regional security. In future, any attack on an American republic by an outside power would be regarded as an attack on them all, with appropriate joint action guaranteed, using force if necessary. This was clearly designed to prevent the confusion of the Second World War, but it did prepare the way for closer co-operation in security matters in the immediate postwar period.

In 1947 the republics all signed the Inter-American Treaty of Reciprocal Assistance (the Rio Treaty), confirming their common policy of defence against outside aggression and pledging themselves to peaceful solutions to disputes between themselves. A year later at Bogotá (Colombia), this was taken one stage further with the creation of the Organisation of American States (OAS), dedicated to the security of the Americas and the forging of economic, social and political links between the member countries.

Many Latin Americans probably presumed that this would lead to increased US financial aid; when it did not, any US hopes of creating a solid anti-communist bloc in the Americas faded. In 1950, when the UN called on its members to send military forces to oppose communist advances in Korea, Colombia was the only Latin American country to respond.

Internal problems

Such a lack of enthusiasm was hardly surprising. Despite the undoubted growth of communist influence in Europe and Asia, and the fear in the United States about its consequences for the "Free World", Latin America was, as yet, relatively unaffected. Communist parties existed in many of the republics, just as they did in the countries of western Europe, but they were poorly organised and politically insignificant.

Of more immediate concern to the Latin American countries in the 1950s were domestic problems arising from continuing social and political rifts, the roots of which went back more than 100 years. Some countries – notably Mexico, Chile and Uruguay – had enjoyed comparative calm, but elsewhere the Second World War had done little to quieten unrest.

Splits between conservatives and liberals still existed, made worse by the steady rise of middle and lower classes desperate for a share of political power. Increased demand for the mineral and agricultural products of Latin America during the war years had led to an economic boom which threatened to undermine the power of traditional ruling élites, chiefly by raising the level of demand for improved living standards and social welfare.

When this was denied or, as happened occasionally, satisfied too quickly by new political parties swept to power by the under-privileged classes, conflict became inevitable. In such circumstances, many Latin American countries became absorbed in their own domestic troubles, caring little about world affairs.

The role of the army

These internal disputes differed from country to country, but in nearly all cases the armed forces (particularly the armies) played a crucial role. They had for long been a major factor in the politics of Latin America, providing the power behind existing rulers or ensuring change by shifting their support to selected rivals.

During the Second World War, that power had been significantly increased as the United States provided weapons and training. The intention was to create forces which would contribute to the Allied war effort; in reality the armed forces improved their ability to intervene in domestic political affairs. Between 1941 and 1961, there were more than 30 successful *coups d'état* in Latin America, resulting in complete changes of government. Many others failed but contributed enormously to political chaos.

Juan and Eva Perón acknowledge the cheers of the people, 1951.

Argentinian developments

This was particularly apparent in Argentina. As early as 1932 a group of military officers used their influence to ensure the election of Agustin Justo, opening the way to a period of ruthless rule known as the "Infamous Decade". This ended in June 1943 when rival officers – the *Grupo de Oficiales Unidos* – intervened, dedicated to the introduction of political ideas based upon those of the fascists in Italy.

Among the new leaders was Colonel Juan Domingo Perón, who began to gather a fanatical following within the working classes of Argentina, particularly when, as head of the Department of Labour, he introduced an advanced social welfare system. He became so popular that when, in October 1945, disgruntled officers engineered his dismissal, he was able to appeal directly to his working-class supporters and have the decision reversed. In fact, when elections were held in February 1946, Perón was swept to power as President of Argentina.

Perón's rule

There followed a decade of *Perónismo* (rule by Perón), in which the president tried to impose his own political doctrine of *Justicialismo* under the slogan "political sovereignty, economic independence, social justice". To many of his followers, he became almost a god, but he also encountered entrenched opposition.

The traditional ruling élite rejected his policy of land reform, which involved the nationalisation (enforced government ownership) and destruction of big estates; the United States distrusted his apparent leanings towards fascism and, when he tried to introduce a divorce law, he came into direct conflict with the Catholic Church.

At the same time, as world demand for Argentinian agricultural products declined in the immediate post-war years, an economic slump set in. This left Perón with little money to maintain his welfare system and forced him to introduce cost-cutting measures which lost him support among the workers and trade unions – the very people who had voted him into office. Finally, many people disliked the way that Perón ruled through favourites, especially when, in 1951, he secured the nomination of his wife Eva as vice-president and his obvious successor.

Eva Perón died in 1952, leaving her husband to cope with mounting economic and political problems. He tried to deal with these by making concessions to the middle classes, hoping that they would counter growing

The image of Perónismo: *Juan and Eva Perón together.*

opposition within the armed forces, but he failed to prevent a series of military and naval revolts which further weakened his grip. Finally, in September 1955, under intense pressure from the armed forces, Perón resigned and fled the country.

Perón was replaced by a military president, Eduardo Lonardi, but he proved unable to control the rising tide of anti-Perón feeling in the army. General Pedro Eugenio Aramburu took over and tried to destroy Perónist influence. He also tried to reintroduce the principle of democratic elections. By then, however, Argentinian society was deeply divided along lines which were guaranteed to cause future trouble: the workers continued to support the memory of Perón; the old ruling class, backed by the armed forces, did all it could to oppose a return to such dangerously popular rule. A period of reactionary government, based on the power of the army, was unavoidable, although this was unlikely to last.

CONFLICT IN THE 20TH CENTURY

Getúlio Vargas (seated, shaking hands) enjoys the enthusiasm of the Brazilian people, 1942.

Vargas in Brazil

In the case of Argentina, the military had played a crucial role in both the rise and fall of Perón, and a similar pattern of intervention may be seen elsewhere in Latin America during the same period. Getúlio Vargas, for example, came to power in Brazil in 1930 as a result of armed revolt, yet lost much of his military support as he tried to introduce working-class reform.

In 1945, he was forced to resign following army pressure, and although Brazil then enjoyed nearly 20 years of "democracy", it was characterised throughout by military involvement in politics, albeit "behind the scenes". Thus, in 1950, Vargas was allowed to return to office only when he promised the army that he would abandon left-wing policies. When Vargas reneged on his promise, the same military men put so much pressure on him that, in 1954, he committed suicide.

The army then openly interfered, taking control of key sectors of administration within successive governments. They feared that reforms would mobilise the workers of Brazil in a popular revolution and lead them to destroy the traditional forms of rule of which the army was an integral part.

Papa Doc and Haiti

Such intervention was, by definition, unconstitutional – after all, armies exist to defend the country, not to rule it – but there were occasions when it was clearly justified if the country was to survive. In Haiti, for example, the army intervened in 1950 and 1956 to prevent the introduction of laws which would have allowed existing presidents to rule indefinitely.

The coups merely produced chaos. Eventually one of the most ruthless dictators of modern Latin America – Dr François ("Papa Doc") Duvalier, came to power. He maintained his rule through a private army known as the *Tontons Macoutes*, renowned for its use of terror to suppress any sign of opposition.

Latin American societies, already split along social and political lines, rarely accepted military rule without some form of reaction. In some instances, the result was a counter-coup by moderate elements of the army determined to restore democracy. This occurred in El Salvador in January 1961, less than a year after left-wing officers under Colonel César Yanez Urias had seized power. Usually the result was civil war and a drift towards dictatorship.

Military coups

This pattern of events was followed with depressing regularity in a variety of Latin American countries. In the Dominican Republic, for example, Rafael Léonidas Trujillo Molina seized power in 1930 at the head of a "National Army", beginning a period of absolute rule which was to last until his assassination in 1961. During that time he expanded the army (and raised an air force) in order to maintain his position, promoted himself to the rank of *Generalissimo* and used terror to prevent the growth of opposition.

On the neighbouring island of Cuba, Fulgencio Batista, an ex-sergeant who had already held power between 1940 and 1944 at the head of a military *junta* (council), returned from self-imposed exile in Florida in 1952, gathered together a group of high-ranking officers (most of whom owed their positions to Batista) and took over. In the process he antagonised the middle classes of the island, and maintained his rule with a reign of terror carried out by the secret police. Civil liberties were suspended, people were arrested, tortured and killed, and opposition groups ruthlessly suppressed.

On the mainland, similar events occurred in Venezuela, where Colonel Marcos Pérez Jiménez held power between 1950 and 1958; in Honduras, where

FROM WORLD WAR TO COLD WAR

SUCCESSFUL MILITARY COUPS SINCE 1945

ARGENTINA 1955 *(2)*, 1962, 1966, 1970, 1976	**DOMINICAN REPUBLIC** 1963, 1965	**NICARAGUA** 1947
BOLIVIA 1946, 1951, 1964, 1969, 1970, 1971, 1978 *(2)*, 1979, 1980, 1981	**ECUADOR** 1947 *(2)*, 1961, 1963, 1966, 1972, 1976	**PANAMA** 1949, 1968
	EL SALVADOR 1948, 1960, 1961, 1979	**PARAGUAY** 1948 *(2)*, 1949, 1954
BRAZIL 1945, 1954, 1964	**GUATEMALA** 1954, 1957, 1963, 1982, 1983	**PERU** 1948, 1962, 1963, 1968, 1975
CHILE 1973	**HAITI** 1946, 1950, 1956	**URUGUAY** 1973, 1976
COLOMBIA 1953, 1957	**HONDURAS** 1954, 1956, 1963, 1972, 1975, 1978	**VENEZUELA** 1945, 1948, 1952, 1958
CUBA 1952		

General Tiburcio Carías ruled with an iron hand between 1933 and 1949; and in Nicaragua, where Anastasio Somoza García, having seized power in 1936, began a family tradition of dictatorship that was to last, through his sons Luis and Anastasio Junior, until 1979 with only a short three-year break in the 1960s. The tradition of the *caudillos* was far from dead.

Rebels in Bolivia, 1952 – a recurring Latin American image.

Alternatives

But there were alternatives. In Mexico, for example, the Revolution of 1910-20 had helped to establish the principle of civilian rule. During the presidency of Lázaro Cárdenas (1934-40) the military's influence was deliberately reduced.

Elsewhere, more drastic solutions to the problem of military intervention were put into effect, sometimes with surprising results. In Bolivia, a right wing military *junta*, acting on behalf of the traditional ruling class (composed principally of wealthy tin-mine owners) was ousted from power in April 1952 by armed militia forces belonging to the National Revolutionary Movement (MNR). Almost immediately, the regular army was downgraded and responsibility for many of its tasks transferred to the militia groups. Officers were sacked, soldiers sent home and weapons concentrated in militia hands. The army was considerably weakened.

In Colombia, where a civil war known as *La Violencia* caused heavy casualties and widespread destruction after 1948, a similar line was adopted. Both the presidency of Rojas Pinilla (1953-57) and support from the United States gradually established the principle of military subordination to civilian rule.

The process was taken to its logical extreme in Costa Rica where, after a two-month civil war in 1948, civilian politicians decided to disband the army entirely, leaving the security of the country in the hands of a more closely controlled Civil Guard. Since then, the Civil Guard has been trained and equipped to carry out most of the duties of a regular army, but the principle of civilian supremacy has been firmly fixed. Many believe that it is the only solution to the problem of military *coups d'état*.

East versus West

Such moves are only possible, however, if the affected country can deal with its problems in its own time, without interference from outside. During the 1950s, most Latin American countries still enjoyed that luxury, but as the decade progressed the affairs of a wider world began to spread to the continent.

This was a direct and inevitable result of the growing confrontation between communism (the "East") and capitalism (the "West") known as the Cold War. Since 1945 the United States had become increasingly aware of the spread of communism, initially in eastern Europe after the end of the Second World War, and then in Asia, with the fall of China to Mao Tse-tung (1949), the Korean War (1950-53) and the emergence of a host of communist-inspired insurgencies.

In such circumstances, the security of Latin America – an area sometimes called the "backyard" of the United States and an essential source of raw materials for the West – began to figure large in US foreign policy. As communism thrived on social unrest and political chaos, Latin America seemed a likely breeding ground. The pattern of interference was established, although the United States did not devote substantial effort to the preservation of anti-communist regimes in the area until the 1960s.

Guatemala

It was shown most obviously in the case of Guatemala, a country sufficiently close to both the United States and the Panama Canal to guarantee the attention of Washington. Before the Second World War, the United States was well satisfied with the political arrangements in Guatemala. In 1931, General Jorge Ubico had seized power and, with US backing, had introduced strong central government.

In the process he alienated the middle classes, elements of the traditional élite and even the army, with the result that political unrest became inevitable. It broke out initially in May 1944, when students in Guatemala City went on strike, protesting about the need for educational reform. As they were joined in essentially peaceful demonstrations by members of the professional and middle class, Ubico fled, leaving a dangerous political vacuum. The students, flushed with success, increased their demands, expressing them through their candidate for the forthcoming presidential election, Juan José Arévalo. His rival, Juan Federico Ponce, chosen by a military *junta* to replace Ubico, responded with repression.

Further revolts

This led to a second revolt, in October 1944, by junior officers of the army under Major Francisco Javier Arana and Captain Jacobo Arbenz Guzman. A temporary *junta* was established and elections held in March 1945: Arévalo became president. Reforms were introduced, but these merely deepened the social and political divides within the country.

A spate of attempted *coups d'état* weakened Arévalo's hold on power and, after Arana was assassinated in 1949, Arbenz emerged as president. He proved to be a dedicated social reformer, but much more worrying for the United States was his close association with the Guatemalan Communist Party.

Washington was sufficiently alarmed to send men of the Central Intelligence Agency (CIA) to make contact with exiled Guatemalans in neighbouring Honduras and, in June 1954, they "invaded" their homeland, led by Colonel Carlos Castillo Armas. Arbenz held the invaders on the border – but as the West would not sell him arms, he turned to the East. It was a foolish move. The CIA stepped up its activities and Arbenz was forced out of office. Armas took over, dedicated to a pro-United States stance.

CIA involvement

Obviously the United States could be well pleased with the outcome of its intervention – a potential communist takeover had been averted and a "friendly" president installed – and Guatemala provided the model for US actions in similar circumstances elsewhere. The role of the CIA was enhanced; economic and military aid was afforded to Latin American regimes (however unsavoury) which seemed to be under pressure from the left.

But the problem did not go away: indeed, as the 1950s progressed, it became steadily worse, reinforcing US fears that the Soviets were intent upon taking the Cold War deep into the Americas. Final proof, if any were needed, came from events in Cuba – the first Latin American country to fall to a communist regime.

Cuban unrest

Opposition to Batista began to emerge almost as soon as he seized power in 1952, taking the form of peaceful demonstrations in favour of a return to democracy. When he responded with repression and terror, the more committed of his opponents turned to violence, attacking selected government targets throughout the island. One of the more spectacular of these attacks

Fidel Castro was the leader of anti-Batista forces in Cuba, 1957.

occurred on 26 July 1953, when about 100 guerrillas stormed the Cuban Army barracks at Moncada.

The guerrillas were forced to surrender. One of their leaders, Fidel Castro, a trained lawyer and dedicated revolutionary, was sentenced to 15 years in prison, although he served less than two. On his release in 1955, he helped to organise a new group, to be known as the 26th July Movement (in memory of the Moncada assault). Eventually, he fled to Mexico, where he gathered a number of fellow exiles and prepared a military operation designed to overthrow Batista.

Castro lands in Cuba

Castro planned to land his men on the southern coast of Cuba, at Santiago de Cuba, at the same time as members of the 26th July Movement, led by Frank País, mounted attacks on government buildings in the town. Unfortunately, the plan misfired. Although País kept his side of the bargain, assaulting a variety of targets in late November 1956, Castro's force of 81 armed men did not arrive aboard the yacht *Granma* until 2 December, by which time Batista had restored order with his usual ruthlessness.

As if that was not enough, Castro came ashore at Las Coloradas, many miles from Santiago de Cuba and, 72 hours later, walked into an army ambush at Alegria del Pio. Only 22 guerrillas survived, forcing Castro to rethink his strategy. With the 26th July Movement scattered and his own force decimated, any chance of seizing power by a co-ordinated military action had clearly disappeared. Also the success of the Alegria del Pio ambush indicated that Batista's troops were aware of the guerrillas' intentions. Contact with the 26th July Movement was quickly restored – País was able to pass food, money, arms and recruits to Castro in early 1957, establishing a link known as *el llano* (the rope) – but direct attacks on Batista's forces were too risky.

Faced with these problems, Castro decided to lead his remaining forces into the sparsely populated Sierra Maestra mountains, on the southeastern coast of Cuba, aiming to set up a base. This was in line with Mao Tse-tung's principle of "revolutionary war" which advocated establishing firm bases of popular support before mounting guerrilla attacks. However, there was little evidence at this stage that Castro was following a deliberate policy of communist insurrection.

His views were left-wing, but he showed little desire to gain the support of the people through the lengthy processes of communist education or indoctrination. Anxious to seize power quickly, he wanted to exploit the widespread grievances of Cuban society, regardless of their political leanings. Since Batista had, in any case, managed to antagonise the landowners, middle classes, students, priests, peasants and even elements of the armed forces by 1957, this was a sensible policy.

The 26th July Movement

But it would be wrong to imagine that Castro achieved success on his own. Without help from the 26th July Movement, his guerrillas would not have survived for long in the Sierra Maestra. País made sure that Batista's forces were diverted by attacks on towns and cities far from Castro's base, giving time for his men (known as *fidelistas*) to recover, recruit and gain experience in the tactics of guerrilla warfare.

It was a long, hard road. By May 1957 Castro still had only 80 active fighters under his command (50 of whom had come from the 26th July Movement). Guerrilla attacks were beginning to affect the morale of regular army patrols sent into the Sierra Maestra, but Batista had little reason to fear for his safety or political position. Indeed, Castro appeared to be so minor a threat that the United States completely underestimated the situation. It was more concerned about the impact of Batista's repression, which was quite clearly alienating vast sectors of the Cuban people. Washington responded by cutting off all military supplies.

Batista rallies his forces

Suddenly recognising the danger, Batista mustered the bulk of his army for a concerted drive into the Sierra Maestra in May 1958, but when this failed to dislodge Castro from his base, the end became inevitable. By then, Castro had begun to get his political message across to the Cuban people, setting up a radio station and printing regular newssheets. Determined to exploit anti-Batista feeling to the full, Castro detached two guerrilla columns, led by Major Camilo Cienfuegos and the Argentinian-born Ernesto "Che" Guevara. They were to open up new fronts in the central provinces of the island, forcing Batista to divide his army to deal with the new threat.

By the end of October 1958, as Las Villas fell to the *fidelistas* and the whole of eastern Cuba, with its valuable sugar plantations, came under Castro's control, Batista faced disaster. Two months later, Guevara seized the communications centre of Placetas and advanced towards Santa Clara. As the demoralised Cuban Army melted away, Batista fled into exile on 1 January 1959, leaving the revolutionaries to enter Havana in triumph, to widespread popular acclaim.

The true nature of Castro's policies became apparent. As proposals for land reform and agricultural nationalisation appeared, it became obvious – not least to the United States which owned many companies there – that the new regime was bent on a course of communism. The Cold War had come to the Caribbean and brought with it changes which were guaranteed to affect the future of Latin America as a whole.

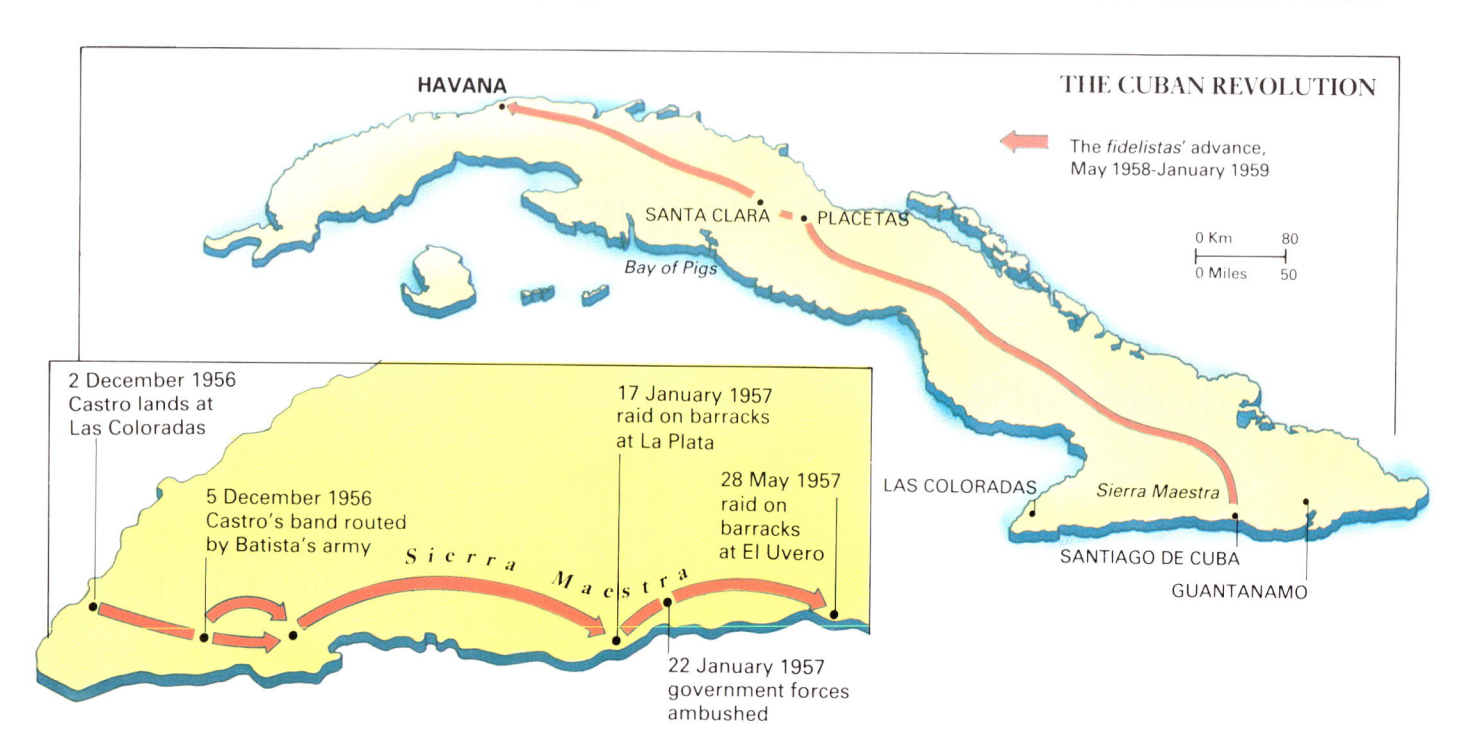

THE CUBAN REVOLUTION

The *fidelistas'* advance, May 1958-January 1959

2 December 1956 Castro lands at Las Coloradas

5 December 1956 Castro's band routed by Batista's army

17 January 1957 raid on barracks at La Plata

28 May 1957 raid on barracks at El Uvero

22 January 1957 government forces ambushed

FROM WORLD WAR TO COLD WAR

Batista (centre) takes power at the head of the military regime in Cuba, 1952.

26 CONFLICT IN THE 20TH CENTURY

CHAPTER 3
GUERRILLAS

With the exception of Cuba itself, the country most directly affected by Castro's victory in early 1959 was the United States. Suddenly to discover that the largest and most important island in the Caribbean had "gone communist" had a profound and far-reaching impact on the government in Washington, led at that time by President Dwight D Eisenhower. His response was to colour US policies towards the region for many years to come.

INSURGENCIES IN SOUTH AND CENTRAL AMERICA

- GUATEMALA 1962-
- EL SALVADOR 1968-
- CUBA 1956-59
- HAITI 1959-60
- HONDURAS
- NICARAGUA 1959-60, 1972-79
- COSTA RICA
- PANAMA
- VENEZUELA 1960-68
- GUYANA
- SURINAM
- FRENCH GUIANA
- COLOMBIA 1964-68
- ECUADOR
- BRAZIL 1969-71
- PERU 1961-65
- BOLIVIA 1967
- PARAGUAY 1959-60
- CHILE 1971-73
- ARGENTINA 1970-76
- URUGUAY 1965-73

In political terms, the events of early 1959 have to be seen as part of the Cold War against the Soviet Union. Since the end of the Second World War in 1945, the deep division between those countries of the West which believed in capitalism (with its emphasis upon freedom and personal choice) and those of the East which embraced communism (based upon strong government control and common ownership of wealth-producing resources had created tension and threats of conflict.

By the late 1950s, this had been confined largely to Europe and the Far East, where communist territorial expansion had taken place. Although the United States had shown itself prepared to take action to prevent the spread of communism into the Americas (most notably in Guatemala in 1954), the ease with which Castro gained power came as something of a shock. If this pattern of revolution could be repeated elsewhere, communism could spread quickly into an area which had been free of its influence up till that time. Castro's success seemed to create a dangerous base, out of which the evil of communism would expand, exploiting the social, political and economic weaknesses of other Latin American countries.

US defences

But there was more to it than that. If such expansion should take place, opening the way to the creation of Soviet military and naval bases in the Caribbean, the security of the United States would be undermined. In the past, the country had enjoyed the advantage of isolation, surrounded by two immense oceans which made direct attack unlikely.

Even if a threat developed, control of the Panama Canal ensured a swift concentration of US forces: if, for example, the enemy appeared on the east coast, warships and military units could be moved from the west with comparative ease. However, if communism should spread, creating a barrier to such freedom of movement, the only alternative would be the long, exposed journey around Cape Horn. Similarly, if countries in Central America (particularly Mexico) followed Castro's lead, it was quite possible that the United States would, for the first time in 100 years, face hostile forces on its land borders. It was not a pleasant prospect.

Finally, the creation of a communist "bloc" in the Caribbean or elsewhere in Latin America would seriously threaten the economy of the United States. In an age of nuclear and military confrontation on a global scale, coinciding with industrial and commercial developments of significant proportions inside the United States, access to the mineral resources and agricultural products of Latin America was vital. If communist expansion in the Caribbean created a barrier to trade or denied resources to US firms, the consequences could be catastrophic. Tobacco and sugar crops had already been lost in Cuba: if the same happened to copper, tin, titanium, lead or iron ore elsewhere in Latin America, the ability of the United States to survive both economically and militarily would be jeopardised.

Isolating Cuba

To begin with, Eisenhower's administration tried to isolate the Cuban threat. As Castro introduced the first of his left-wing policies, nationalising US assets on the island, US firms were ordered to cease trading with Cuba. It was hoped this would weaken the regime.

At the same time, the United States used its influence in the OAS to persuade the rest of Latin America to break off diplomatic relations with Cuba, refusing to recognise Castro's government. Some success was achieved – by the early 1960s, Castro was facing deep economic problems and had failed to find support from his Latin American neighbours – but this seemed to do nothing to destroy the appeal of communism inside Cuba: indeed, as a direct result of the pressures, Castro was already looking for aid from the Soviet Union, skilfully playing one superpower off against the other.

Anti-Castro plans

The most obvious move would have been to mount an invasion of Cuba using the overwhelming military power of the United States. But with the Cold War at its height such overt action was fraught with danger. Instead, Eisenhower decided to repeat the pattern established in Guatemala, using the CIA to train and equip Cuban exiles (many of whom were living in Florida) to "liberate" their homeland, closely supported by the United States.

Under the direction of Richard Bissell, CIA Deputy Director of Plans, a Cuban "government-in-exile" was to be created, backed by a covert radio station designed to beam anti-Castro propaganda to the island. The intention was to use Castro's own proven methods to ensure his overthrow: as the guerrillas entered Cuba, they would be supported by a network of sympathisers in a society already weakened by economic problems and anti-Castro propaganda.

The Bay of Pigs

Unfortunately for the anti-Castro forces, the plan was put together too quickly. The size of the invasion force was increased without checking the loyalty of new recruits. The creation of training and supply bases in Guatemala and Nicaragua could not be kept secret for long and, because of the presidential elections in November 1960, Eisenhower insisted on leaving the role of US forces vague, for fear of a public outcry.

When President John F Kennedy inherited the scheme in early 1961, he ruled that US forces should not be directly involved. He was prepared to provide a naval escort for the invasion fleet as it moved towards Cuba and to turn a blind eye to the fact that members of the Alabama National Guard had been recruited to fly B-26 bombers in support of the landings. But if it all went wrong, he could deny direct US involvement.

Survivors of "Brigade 2506" are rounded up, Bay of Pigs, 1961.

"Brigade 2506", comprising about 1,300 Cuban exiles, landed at Giron in the Bay of Pigs, on the southern coast of Cuba, on 17 April 1961. The operation was a complete disaster. Preliminary bomber attacks failed to destroy Castro's air force and, without realising it, the "invaders" came ashore in an area well known to the Cuban leader. He took immediate control, leading his troops in counterattacks which contained and then destroyed the invading force. Nikita Khrushchev, the Soviet premier, offered "every assistance" to Castro, and Kennedy, aware that a superpower confrontation might develop, refused to authorise any US military moves. By 19 April, Brigade 2506 had ceased to exist.

The Cuban Missile Crisis

The consequences were far-reaching. Inside Cuba, Castro used the reality of invasion as an excuse to arrest all those who stood in the way of a fully fledged communist regime, and thereafter he made little attempt to disguise his left-wing intentions. More dramatically, the events of April 1961 placed Cuba firmly in the Soviet camp, opening the way to an even greater crisis as Khrushchev exploited the geographic location of his new ally.

His offer of support had not been made unconditionally, for it soon became obvious that the price was the creation of Soviet bases on the island, only 145 km (90 miles) from the United States. By July 1962, Kennedy was aware of military activity around Havana and when, three months later, U-2 reconnaissance aircraft brought back photographs of Soviet missile sites under construction, the nightmare of direct nuclear attack on US cities had to be faced.

Kennedy, by now a much more confident president, responded by imposing a blockade around Cuba. He also threatened the Soviets with military action if the missiles were deployed, and during 13 days of crisis (16-28 October 1962), it looked as if a major superpower war would break out. Khrushchev recognised the danger and backed down, but the true nature of US fears about communist expansion in Latin America had been highlighted. The prevention of such expansion has been a priority of US foreign policy ever since.

Exporting revolution

Such a reaction was more than justified in the early 1960s for, as the Bay of Pigs and Cuban Missile Crisis occurred, Castro was actively pursuing the idea of "exporting" his revolution elsewhere in Latin America. His victory in 1959 seemed to suggest that he had created a "model" for success, geared specifically to the needs and realities of Latin American politics.

By the early 1960s, this model had been analysed and refined, chiefly through the writings of Che Guevara. Three basic "lessons" emerged. According to Guevara, the Cuban experience showed that Latin American dictators like Batista were extremely vulnerable to pressure, not least because they could not depend upon the loyalty of their armed forces; that rural-based revolution, mobilising the power of the ordinary peasants, was guaranteed to succeed by sheer weight of numbers; and that, in such circumstances, the role of the revolutionary leadership, acting as a "focus" for popular discontent, was crucial.

In other words, regardless of political events, all that was needed to ensure communist victory was the appearance of dedicated revolutionaries. These would exploit existing grievances and expose the vulnerability of dictators whose hold on power was tenuous, depending as it did on the use of force. Known as the *foco* theory, it was an attractive analysis.

Problems with Guevara's theory

But the model was false. Although it undoubtedly applied to events in Cuba between 1956 and 1959, there was no guarantee that the same situation would arise elsewhere. Indeed, in too many ways, the Cuban revolt was unique: Batista was already isolated and weak when Castro arrived on the scene, having alienated key sectors of Cuban society by his authoritarian rule; the Cuban Army was never completely dedicated to its task of protecting the dictator, preferring if at all possible to avoid direct contact with the *fidelistas*.

At the same time, Guevara's analysis, with its emphasis upon rural-based revolution, conveniently ignored the role of the 26th July Movement and its essentially urban structure. Castro's comment that "the city is the graveyard of the guerrilla" may have contained an element of truth, but it totally misjudged the reality of urbanisation (the growth of cities) in many Latin American countries.

Any attempt to spread the message of communist revolution through the Cuban model was therefore fraught with problems, most of which became apparent between 1961 and 1968 – the so-called "period of revolutionary reverses". Castro's victory in 1959 had led to a number of "copycat" insurrections – notably in Nicaragua, Haiti and Paraguay – but these were minor and easily contained by local armed forces.

A US nightmare takes shape: aerial photos of a Soviet missile site on Cuba, 1962.

Guerrilla surge

The real surge of guerrilla activity came after it was apparent that Castro had survived the full force of "Yankee imperialism", manifested in the Bay of Pigs and the economic blockade. This was the inspiration needed by the guerrillas. But despite attempts by Castro to co-ordinate support for their activities – in 1966 he convened a Tricontinental Conference in Havana, with representatives from China, the Soviet Union and the Third World – none of the revolutionary groups was successful.

Revolutionary groups

In many ways, this was surprising, for the groups involved seemed to have firm roots among the people and were usually led by charismatic commanders. Both the FARC (*Fuerzas Armadas Revolucionarias Colombianas*) and ELN (*Ejército de Liberación Nacional*) in Colombia, for example, had their origins in peasant republics set up during the civil war of the late 1940s, and the latter, led by the ex-priest Camilo Torres, was able to command a substantial following. The same was true in Peru, where the FIR (*Frente de Izquierda Revolucionaria*) was commanded by Hugo Blanco.

Guatemala and Venezuela

In Guatemala the FAR (*Fuerzas Armadas Rebeldes*) and MR-13 (*Movimiento Revolucionario 13 de Noviembre*) were both set up by ex-officers in the aftermath of an abortive *coup d'état* in November 1960. Even in Venezuela, where the election of a reforming president, Rómulo Betancourt, in 1958 should have undermined popular support for guerrilla insurgency, the MIR (*Movimiento de Izquierda Revolucionaria*) was by no means an isolated or unpopular group. Yet by 1968 all such organisations and most of their leaders had been destroyed.

The Bolivian revolution

To understand why this should be, it is best to look at one particular "revolution" in detail. Of all the revolutionary attempts of the mid-1960s, the one in Bolivia in 1967 should have stood a good chance of success, if only because it was organised and led by a proven guerrilla commander, Che Guevara.

His role in the Cuban revolt, where he had led a guerrilla column into Havana, and his subsequent analysis of Castro's success had ensured him a place in the history books. But he was convinced that Cuba was merely the beginning of a process of revolution designed to sweep aside the injustices of Latin American society. He was realistic enough to recognise that any such attempt would alienate the United States (he had seen what could happen in 1954, when he had tried to support Arbenz in Guatemala) and he worked out a strategy accordingly.

By 1966, having found political life in Cuba frustrating, he decided to mount a guerrilla campaign in Bolivia (chosen because of its central position, bordering five other Latin American countries) which would drag the United States into a long drawn-out and costly war, not unlike that taking place in Vietnam, and mobilise the people in a common hatred of their northern neighbour. Using the *foco* theory, Guevara believed that a small band of dedicated revolutionaries could appear in Bolivia, attracting support from wide sections of a discontented population and creating the mood for change.

Setbacks for Guevara

But Guevara prepared himself and his group badly, failing to appreciate the realities of Bolivian political life. By 1966, President René Barrientos had been in power for two years, and although he had gained office initially by means of a military *coup d'état*, he had only recently received substantial popular support in reasonably free and fair elections. More to the point, he had already introduced land reform, designed to make the peasants owners of the soil they worked: indeed, in Santa Cruz province, where Guevara chose to begin his revolution, local people could literally lay claim to as much land as they required.

In such circumstances, any attempt by Guevara to gain support by the usual communist cry of "land to the tiller" was not likely to have much effect. Furthermore Guevara's group – comprising only 17 hand-picked Cuban guerrillas – failed to learn the right Amerindian dialect for the region, leaving them unable to communicate with the very people they had come to "liberate". It soon became obvious that they would become isolated and vulnerable to military response. As strangers in Bolivia, the guerrillas stood out anyway, and when they found that they could command little support (in all, only 20 Bolivians actually joined the group), their chances of success were slim.

The final fiasco

Guevara arrived at La Paz (the capital of Bolivia) disguised as a Uruguayan businessman, on 3 November 1966. He immediately travelled to a farm at Nancahuazú, deep in the surrounding countryside, where he joined the rest of his small group. Their isolation soon became apparent – even the local Communist Party, insulted by Guevara's presumption that he knew best, deserted him – and the group could do little to spread their beliefs among a scattered and alien population.

In March 1967, Guevara led his guerrillas away from Nancahuazú on a "training march", and the problems grew worse. Many of his group were unfit and had not been prepared for the gruelling countryside of Bolivia. Guevara himself, an asthma sufferer, found the going particularly hard. Struggling back to their base camp, the group became split and, as local peasants betrayed them to the authorities, elements of the Bolivian Army closed in.

Despite mounting an effective ambush, Guevara and the main party were gradually surrounded by superior forces which, by late September, included a US-trained Ranger battalion. On 8 October, the guerrillas were attacked close to the Rio Grande river. After a rather one-sided firefight, Guevara was wounded and captured. The following morning, on the orders of President Barrientos, he was executed and his body put on public display.

Problems of *foco* theory

The Bolivian "revolution" had ended disastrously, for several reasons. Guevara and his ill-prepared group were strangers in a harsh land; they failed to win the support of the local people and they misread the realities of Bolivian politics. Unlike Cuba, where Batista was already well hated by the time Castro began his campaign, Barrientos was reasonably popular. He enjoyed the support of the army and the Church.

In such circumstances, the *foco* theory stood little chance of success, lacking the deep-rooted discontents it needed to create a momentum for change. In addition, of course, Castro's victory in Cuba acted as a warning to politicians elsewhere in Latin America, so that any trouble in rural areas, instead of being ignored or dismissed as "bandit" activity, was sure to elicit a response, denying the revolutionaries the time they needed to spread their message and gain support. In short, the Cuban model just did not apply.

Alliance for Progress

But there was one other factor of equal, if not overwhelming importance, highlighted in the closing stages of the Bolivian fiasco. It was not only local politicians who were forewarned of the communist threat. The United States also recognised the danger and did all it could to support existing regimes.

As early as 1961, in response to Khrushchev's announcement that the Soviets would aid "national liberation" movements worldwide, Kennedy introduced his "Alliance for Progress", aimed specifically at Latin America. Money, arms and expertise were offered to any member of the OAS under communist pressure, with the intention of allowing them to create "civic-military" programmes designed to ensure a measure of popular support for the existing government. US Special Forces ("Green Berets") were encouraged by Kennedy to explore the full potential of counter-insurgency (COIN) techniques.

Che Guevara in Bolivia, 1967.

CONFLICT IN THE 20TH CENTURY

The Dominican Republic

But this not the full extent of US action. Events in the Dominican Republic in 1965 showed how President Lyndon B Johnson (Kennedy's successor) was prepared to commit main-force military units to prevent communist takeovers in selected circumstances. In this particular case, the trouble began in 1961, when the Dominican president Rafael Trujillo was assassinated. Although he was replaced by a moderate left-winger, Juan Bosch, political stability had been lost.

Bosch was overthrown in a military *coup d'état* in 1963, but the new *junta* was itself a victim of military revolt two years later, when rebel forces under Colonel Francisco Caamaño invited Bosch to return from exile to set up a constitutional government. They were opposed by units loyal to the old *junta* and a virtual civil war ensued. On the face of it, this was just one more chapter in the long-running saga of Latin American instability. However, as reports of communist activity among Caamaño's forces were received, the United States became alarmed.

Inter-American Peace Force

The last thing that Johnson wanted was another Cuba and, under the pretence of protecting US nationals trapped by the fighting in Santo Domingo (the capital of the Dominican Republic), he ordered US Marines to go ashore. They landed on 28 April 1965, but failed to halt the momentum of popular support in favour of Caamaño.

Johnson responded by reinforcing the Marines, building up his military strength until, in early May, he had over 3,000 men available for more positive action. On 2 May, the Marines advanced from their base at San Isidro into Santo Domingo – a distance of about 19 km (12 miles). As the US presence grew to a staggering 32,000 service personnel, backed by small contingents from Brazil, Honduras, Nicaragua, Paraguay and Costa Rica, a special OAS Inter-American Peace Force was set up, forcing the Dominican rivals to settle their differences.

By August, a compromise had been agreed and Hector García Godoy was appointed provisional president pending democratic elections in 1966. When these took place in June, Dr Joaquin Balaguer assumed office at the head of a moderate, pro-United States government and all foreign forces were withdrawn. At a cost of 24 US servicemen killed, a communist takeover had been prevented and a precedent of armed intervention, under the banner of the OAS, established.

Men of the US 101st Airborne Division round up suspects in Santo Domingo, May 1965.

Revolutionary climate

Despite the success of US responses, however, the threat of communist insurgency in Latin America did not disappear. The Cuban model of revolution may have been discredited by 1968 and the idea of rural-based guerrilla campaigns effectively countered, but the insurgents did not give up their dream. As the rural movements came under pressure, many revolutionary leaders mounted attacks on government targets in the cities, hoping to divert attention (and forces) away from the countryside so that "safe bases" could be established and popular support built up.

In many ways, this was a dangerous move, bringing the guerrillas into direct confrontation with government forces in areas which the latter were sure to protect. But there were compensations: the cities contained a mass of targets, not all of which could be

Social problems

The reasons were twofold: a population "explosion" and a failure of traditional agricultural economies in many Latin American countries. In Uruguay, for example, world demand for wool declined in the late 1950s, prices slumped and unemployment rose, just at a time when social welfare schemes were producing a growth in population figures, reducing infant-mortality rates and lengthening average life-spans. As the land could no longer satisfy the needs of the people, many moved to the capital, Montevideo, in search of work, money and food, and this was a pattern repeated elsewhere in Latin America. It would have been fine if the cities had been demanding cheap labour because of industrialisation, but this was not the case.

As families drifted away from the countryside, they found none of the things they required – no work, no money, no food and no housing – and many were forced to build shacks of corrugated iron or even cardboard boxes for shelter. Huge "shanty towns" grew up around the cities – by 1970, for example, anyone approaching Montevideo had to pass through a "misery belt" up to 32 km (20 miles) deep – and, as the governments could not cope, an enormous well of discontent was created.

At the same time, population figures continued to rise – by the late 1960s two out of every five people in Latin America were under the age of 15 – and the ranks of the discontented unemployed mushroomed. It was just what the revolutionaries needed and just what they had failed to find in the rural areas. A shift to urban guerrilla warfare, originally designed merely to relieve the pressure on rural campaigns, rapidly became important in its own right.

Urban guerrillas

Urban warfare was nothing new – it had been used by the Irish against the British as early as 1916 and, more recently, by the Algerians against the French between 1954 and 1962. But the Latin American revolutionaries of the late 1960s brought it up to date, tapping the traditions of urban revolt that had for long been a characteristic of their region and making it an integral part of the process of left-wing insurgency. They even produced their own theorist of urban guerrilla warfare – Carlos Marighela, a Brazilian activist whose book, *The Minimanual of Urban Guerrilla Warfare*, was to become the "bible" of the new revolutionaries – as well as a rash of campaigns designed to overthrow existing governments.

defended adequately. The guerrillas could hide in the maze of city streets and, of course, any success such as the destruction of an important building or the assassination of a leading personality was guaranteed to receive maximum publicity, suggesting government weakness and helping to create a "climate of collapse".

More significantly, as many revolutionaries discovered in the late 1960s, the cities contained enormous numbers of people desperate for social and political change. While the rural insurgencies had been taking place, much of Latin America had undergone a revolution of a different kind, epitomised by a massive shift of population away from the countryside and into the urban centres. According to some estimates, by 1966 Latin America as a whole had gone 50 per cent urban – half the entire population was living in or around the cities – and this figure continued to rise as the decade progressed.

"Safe bases"

The aim in all of these was to provoke a political and social crisis through guerrilla and, increasingly, terrorist action, forcing the government to respond in ways which would alienate the people. Small groups of fighters, using the shanty towns as "safe bases" and the discontented masses as their support, would mount attacks specifically to humiliate the government, weakening its hold on the country preparatory to popular uprisings led by the revolutionaries. As a theory, it seemed to make sense.

It did not work in practice, chiefly because it ignored the traditional role of armed forces in the politics of Latin America. In Brazil, for example, an urban campaign began in 1969, but made little headway against a firmly entrenched military *junta* which had been in power since the overthrow of President João Goulart five years earlier. Opposition to the *junta* had always been fragmented, and the campaign was, in fact, the work of two rival revolutionary groups – the VPR (*Vanguarde Popular Revolucionária*), under Carlos Lamarca, and the ALN (*Acção Libertadora Nacional*), led by Carlos Marighela.

Lamarca, a renegade army officer, was first on the scene, mounting a series of attacks on government buildings in January 1969, but it was a group associated with Marighela's ALN which gained maximum publicity when, in September, they kidnapped the US ambassador, Charles Burke Elbrick, forcing the Brazilian government to release 15 convicted or suspected terrorists from gaol in exchange. But the campaign was short-lived. On 4 November 1969, Marighela was shot during a bank robbery, having been betrayed by two Dominican friars under torture, and this degree of government ruthlessness became the norm. In 1970 the ALN was virtually wiped out and, in August 1971, Lamarca was similarly betrayed and shot.

To ensure that the problem did not re-emerge, the Brazilian *junta* ordered mass arrests of suspects, authorised a use of torture and ignored the actions of "death squads" such as the CCC (*Comando Caça Communista*) and OBAN (*Operação Bandeirantes*), which roamed the streets, murdering anyone suspected of left-wing sympathies. By 1973, guerrilla activity had ceased and the population had been intimidated into silence.

The Tupamaros

A similar pattern of events occurred in Uruguay. However, there the urban guerrilla campaign which began in the late 1960s, did so against a liberal democratic regime. The MLN (*Movimiento de Libera-*

The end of the Allende regime, 1973: as soldiers patrol the streets . . .

ción Nacional), more popularly known as the Tupamaros, had its origins among left-wing trade unions, gaining widespread working-class and student support as the existing government failed to cope with a rising tide of economic and social problems. Kidnappings, bank raids and attacks on police and army barracks gradually forced the government to introduce repressive counter-measures, controlling the press and banning certain left-wing political parties, but this merely increased the appeal of the Tupamaros.

In 1970, the guerrillas shifted the emphasis of their campaign, murdering Dan Mitrione, a US official on loan to the Uruguayan police, and kidnapping the British ambassador to Uruguay, Geoffrey Jackson, who was to be held until September 1971 and released only after a spectacular prison break by more than 100 Tupamaros suspects. By then, significant sectors of the population had lost confidence in the government.

In November 1971, presidential elections brought Juan María Bordaberry to power, dedicated to the destruction of the Tupamaros. On 15 April 1972, he declared a state of "internal war" and, as the army gradually assumed responsibility for law and order, civil liberties virtually disappeared. By June, Congress had been dissolved, an army-run National Security Council had been set up in its place and a campaign of government terror against the guerrillas had begun. The familiar pattern of mass arrests, torture and intimidation soon emerged, during which the Tupamaros were wiped out, along with most of the trappings of democracy.

The military hit back

By the early 1970s, the governments of Latin America were increasingly right-wing and repressive. Few liberal democracies proved strong enough to withstand the enormous pressures created by population growth, economic failure and guerrilla activity. Many reverted to their previous traditions of dictatorship and military rule. In this, they were often encouraged by the actions of the United States, determined to prevent the emergence of communist governments.

In September 1973, for example, the democratically elected Marxist President of Chile, Salvador Allende, was overthrown and killed in a military *coup d'état* which was widely believed to have been engineered by the CIA, bringing to power one of the most ruthless dictators of the modern world, General Augusto Pinochet. Elsewhere – in Paraguay, Haiti, Nicaragua, Brazil and Uruguay – Washington did nothing to prevent the establishment of regimes dedicated to authoritarian rule.

. . .suspects are rounded up and taken to a soccer stadium.

Repression has begun.

Pro-Perónist demonstration, Buenos Aires, 1985.

CHAPTER 4
IDEOLOGICAL ARENA

The impact of guerrilla activity was felt most strongly in Argentina, affecting both regional and international affairs into the 1980s. By then, a trend towards democracy had begun to appear in the continent as a whole. However, crises especially in Central America continued to arise, alarming the United States and producing further tension, particularly as communism still seemed to be spreading.

Despite the overthrow of Juan Perón in 1955, his memory had remained strong among the lower classes of Argentina. This was particularly true in the 1960s as the country went through a series of economic crises, brought on in part by a decline in the world demand for Argentinian beef. Successive military governments proved unable to control inflation or to introduce the sorts of social reform promised by Perón.

In May 1969, an uprising in the city of Cordoba showed the depth of public despair. This social turmoil produced the guerrillas. The main groups to turn to violence were the ERP (*Ejército Revolucionario del Pueblo*), holding extreme left-wing views based on the writings of the Russian revolutionary Lev Trotsky, and the Montoneros, a pro-Perónist faction dedicated to the doctrine of *Justicialismo*.

Perón returns
Both groups specialised in the tactics of assassination and kidnap, concentrating on representatives of the military *junta* and its foreign backers. Vast sums of money (a reported $14 million in the case of an Esso executive in March 1974) were demanded for the release of kidnap victims, who were murdered if the

ransom was not paid. The level of violence caught the authorities unprepared and, after a succession of ineffective generals had failed to restore order, presidential elections were called in May 1973.

The *Justicialista* (Perónist) Party won a clear majority in the National Congress and Dr Hector Cámpora assumed control, only to step down in favour of Perón when the latter returned from exile. Perón was elected president in October 1973, with his second wife, Isabelita, as vice-president. Hopes that this would end the guerrillas' campaign quickly faded. The ERP distrusted Perón and the Montoneros were already demanding reforms well to the left of those promised by the new government. The violence continued.

Another coup

Perón died in July 1974 and was replaced immediately by Isabelita. She was incapable of providing the strong leadership so desperately needed, depending more and more upon the advice of her late husband's secretary, Lopez Rega. As rumours of corruption increased, she responded by suspending the National Congress, only to provoke yet another military *coup d'état*, in March 1976. By then, the ERP had extended its guerrilla campaign to the countryside – in the summer of 1975, an entire army brigade had been needed to secure control of Tucuman province. The Montoneros had also stepped up their policy of political assassination, including (in January 1975) the shooting down of an aircraft carrying members of the Army General Staff.

Disappearances

Once back in power the armed forces, headed by General Jorge Videla, responded to the guerrillas with a ruthlessness that was soon to become notorious as the "Dirty War". The pattern was not unusual: as in Brazil and Uruguay, civil rights were suspended and violence and terror were used. Right-wing death squads, such as the AAA (*Alianza Anticommunista Argentina*), murdered known left-wingers.

Riots in Cordoba, Argentina, 1969.

Protest at the "Dirty War", Plazo de Mayo, Buenos Aires.

No one knows for sure how many people died – estimates vary between 7,000 and 15,000 – but vast numbers "disappeared", often into torture centres run by the armed forces or police. For a time, this led to increased guerrilla activity, but by 1977 the sheer weight of government repression had driven the ERP and Montoneros deep underground. The only public signs of disquiet occurred every Thursday, when the mothers of those who had "disappeared" demonstrated silently in the Plaza de Mayo in Buenos Aires.

Economic problems

None of this solved the underlying problems of Argentina. In a situation of collapsing exports and an annual inflation rate of 600 per cent, the *junta* began to feel the strain. Videla resigned the presidency in March 1981, having failed to restore democracy. He was succeeded by General Roberto Viola, although it soon became obvious that the real power lay elsewhere. In December 1981 the presidency was transferred to army strong-man Leopoldo Galtieri, apparently secure in the support of the air force and navy representatives on the ruling council, Brigadier Basilio Lami Dozo and Admiral Jorge Anaya.

They could do little to control the economic situation, however, and as riots became an almost daily occurrence on the streets of the capital, they searched for something that would divert public attention while at the same time boosting their own popularity. They found it in the issue of the Malvinas, a group of islands 480 km (300 miles) off the coast of Argentina known more generally as the Falklands.

Administered by Britain since 1833 but subject to Spanish claims (inherited by Argentina) which dated back to the 1760s, the Falklands had for long been a source of intense Argentinian nationalist fervour: if Galtieri and his fellow rulers could seize control of the islands, many of the country's problems would be forgotten in the euphoria of popular acclaim.

The Falklands factor

This was a tempting proposition, made more so by two other factors. First, the new administration in the United States, under President Ronald Reagan, had already shown a willingness to improve relations with Argentina. These had been soured when Reagan's predecessor, Jimmy Carter, had cut off military aid because of the "Dirty War".

Second, Prime Minister Margaret Thatcher's government in London had announced defence cuts in June 1981. These included the withdrawal from the South Atlantic of the ice-patrol vessel HMS *Endurance*, Britain's only permanent naval presence in the area. The likelihood of an armed response to an invasion seemed remote. It was clearly a gamble worth taking.

The Argentinian invasion

The Argentinian attack on Port Stanley, the capital of the Falklands, began at 0420 hours (local time) on 2 April 1982, and the defending force of only 79 Royal Marines was quickly overwhelmed. Twenty-four hours later, the Falklands dependency of South Georgia, 1,290 km (800 miles) to the east-south-east, was also seized.

Amid scenes of wild jubilation in Buenos Aires, the political and economic problems of Argentina were temporarily overshadowed; Galtieri and his fellow *junta*-members were hailed as national heroes and, for a time, it looked as if a major victory had been achieved, at virtually no cost.

Galtieri (left) visits General Menendez, Falklands, 1982.

Britain fights back

But Galtieri had misjudged his opponent. Within a matter of hours, Britain had responded with a formidable package of counter-measures, designed to put maximum pressure on the Argentinians. In the United Nations Security Council, skilful diplomatic moves ensured the adoption of Resolution 502 on 3 April, condemning the Argentinian action and calling on both sides to seek a peaceful solution to the Falklands question.

At the same time, Argentinian bank accounts and credit facilities in Britain were closed and trading links severed. Britain also persuaded her European allies to do the same. Finally, and most unexpectedly from the Argentinian point of view, Mrs Thatcher authorised the creation of a naval "task force" and its movement towards the South Atlantic (a distance of 13,000 km/ 8,000 miles), with the obvious intention of regaining possession of the islands by force if all else failed.

The first units, including the aircraft carriers HMS *Hermes* and *Invincible*, loaded with Royal Marines, helicopters and Sea Harrier "jump-jets", left Portsmouth on 5 April. They were followed by specially chartered transports carrying paratroops and yet more marines (together constituting 3rd Commando Brigade). A 320-km (200-mile) Maritime Exclusion Zone (MEZ) was imposed by the British around the Falklands a week later, policed by nuclear-powered submarines.

The United States backs Britain

Meanwhile, the Argentinians had reinforced their garrison on the Falklands to a strength of 10,000 men, commanded by Major-General Mario Menendez, and turned to their own allies for support. They fully expected the OAS to back their actions, or at least to oppose any British moves into a region protected by the Rio Treaty of 1947, but when a meeting of the republics took place on 26 April, the response was only lukewarm. Four days later, the United States finally chose to back Britain rather than Argentina, despite the obvious implications for American solidarity in the future.

Argentinian defeats

Events in the South Atlantic were going against the Argentinians. On 25 April, British forces had retaken South Georgia and on 1 May the main attack on the Falklands began, with air strikes against the airfield at Port Stanley.

CONFLICT IN THE 20TH CENTURY

Sinking the *Belgrano*

Twenty-four hours later, the Argentinian cruiser *General Belgrano* was torpedoed and sunk with the loss of 368 lives, heralding the start of a serious military confrontation. The Argentinian Navy, clearly outclassed, withdrew to its home ports, but the Air Force, operating at the extremes of its range from bases in Argentina, sought out the task force. On 4 May the destroyer HMS *Sheffield* was damaged beyond repair by a French-supplied Exocet sea-skimming missile.

British landing

This particular attack demonstrated the vulnerability of the British force and made an assault on the Falklands vital. As reinforcements set sail from England, some of them on board the liner *Queen Elizabeth 2*, preparations for a landing were made. After much deliberation, 3rd Commando Brigade went ashore on East Falkland on 21 May, although not where the Argentinians had expected: instead of at Port Stanley, which Menendez had defended in depth, the landing took place on the opposite side of the island, at Port San Carlos. The Argentinians were caught looking the wrong way.

The Argentinian Air Force responded with attack after attack on British shipping protecting the landing force. Despite heavy losses, the pilots succeeded in hitting the frigate HMS *Ardent* on 21 May, followed two days later by her sister-ship HMS *Antelope*; on the 25th the destroyer HMS *Coventry* was sunk, along with the requisitioned container-ship *Atlantic Conveyor*.

Only when the attacks diminished did the British break out from their beachhead. On 27 May, a battalion of paratroops (2PARA) advanced south to take Darwin and Goose Green (where they fought an epic battle on 28/29 May to capture both settlements), while 3PARA and 45 Commando, Royal Marines, marched across the island towards Port Stanley. By 1 June, as the reinforcements from England came ashore, British troops had taken Mount Kent and Mount Challenger, overlooking Port Stanley. Menendez had lost the strategic initiative.

After a brief period of consolidation (during which Argentinian aircraft carried out a devastating attack on the landing ships *Sir Tristram* and *Sir Galahad* at Fitzroy), the British closed in on the capital. During the night of 11/12 June, their troops took the hill features known as Two Sisters, Harriet and Longdon; two

Argentinian troops in Port Stanley, Falklands, 1982.

THE FALKLANDS WAR, APRIL–JUNE 1982

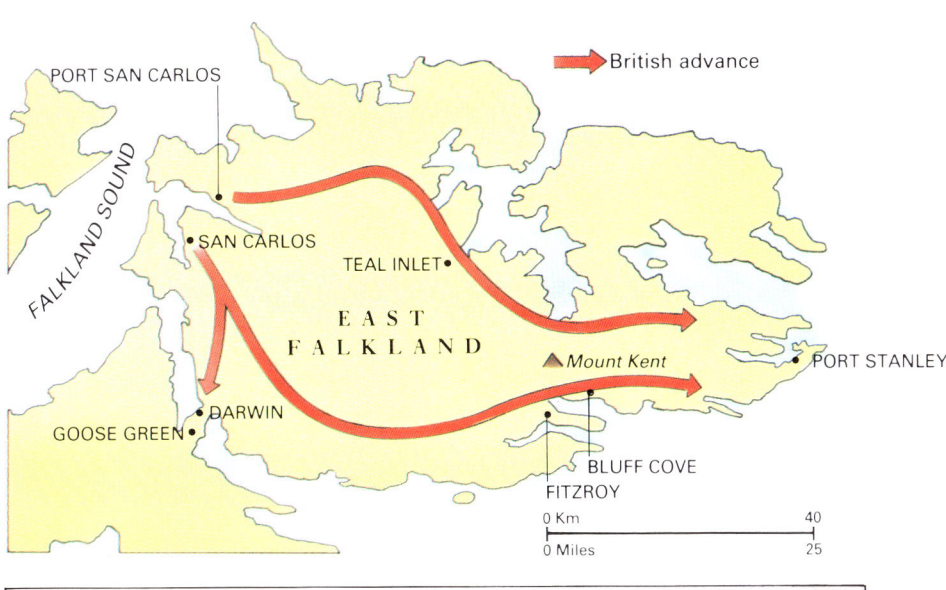

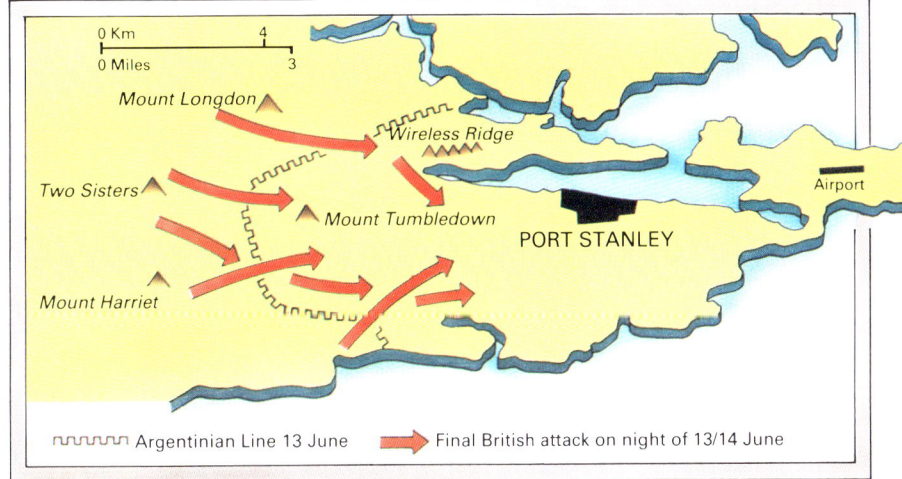

Despite the distance from the UK, British troops liberated the Falklands in May–June 1982, chiefly by surprising the Argentinians with a landing at Port San Carlos and rapid march on Port Stanley.

nights later, they seized Mount Tumbledown and Wireless Ridge. The fighting was hard, in deteriorating winter conditions. Despite problems of morale among Argentinian troops in some areas, in others the defenders fought well, but by 14 June, with the high ground firmly in British hands, Menendez was forced to surrender. The 14-week war had cost the Argentinians about 760 dead; the British lost 255.

The return to democracy

The consequences of the Argentinian defeat were profound. As Britain continued to exert diplomatic and economic pressure, trying (and failing) to force a permanent settlement of the Falklands question, public anger in Buenos Aires turned against the ruling *junta*. Galtieri resigned, but this was not enough to satisfy the people.

In October 1983, presidential elections were held, out of which emerged a new civilian government, headed by Raúl Alfonsín. He began to impose his authority in a variety of ways. Political prisoners were released and those members of the armed forces responsible for conducting the "Dirty War" were put on trial. At the same time, relations with Chile were improved by accepting the mediation of the Vatican in a long-running dispute over ownership of the islands of Picton, Lennox and Nueva in the Beagle Channel to the south of Tierra del Fuego (the Beagle Channel Treaty, October 1984).

Settlement of foreign disputes coupled with the failure of the armed forces in the Falklands meant a loss of prestige by the military in Argentina. This provoked a backlash from officers used to political power. In April 1987, a series of military revolts shook the government, but Alfonsín stood firm. However, with many of the social and economic problems of Argentina still unresolved, he had to struggle to survive politically.

Decline of the dictators

Argentina was not alone in experiencing a return to democracy. In Uruguay, elections held in November 1984 resulted in the installation of Julio Sanguinetti as the first civilian president since 1973; two months later, Brazil followed suit, electing Tancredo Neves to the presidency, and although he died before he could take office, there was a smooth transfer of power to his vice-president, José Sarney.

Even well-established dictators were ousted. In February 1986, for example, "Baby Doc" Duvalier, who had succeeded his father "Papa Doc" as president of Haiti in 1971, was forced to flee (although he was replaced by a military council under General Henri Namphy). Other dictators came under new pressures from populations tired of ineffective government responses to the persistent problems of mounting debt and social hardship.

By 1987, only two hard-line *caudillos* remained in power in Latin America – Alfredo Stroessner (by then 75 years old) in Paraguay and Augusto Pinochet in Chile. Although less-than-liberal regimes still existed, the demand for change was widely apparent.

The violence beneath

But this did not mean that the traditions of Latin American politics had disappeared: far from it. In Uruguay, for example, Sanguinetti faced growing pressure from the armed forces, who retained the "right" to intervene if civilian rule should be seen to fail. This centred on the issue of an amnesty for officers held responsible for torture and repression during the campaign against the Tupamaros.

Meanwhile, in Peru, where Alan García was elected president in July 1985, left-wing guerrillas of the *Sendero Luminoso* (Shining Path) conducted a campaign reminiscent of that carried out by the ERP or Montoneros in Argentina a decade earlier. In 1986 alone, guerrillas attacked a hydroelectric power complex, planted bombs in the capital, Lima, and assassinated selected members of the armed forces.

In response, despite García's professed liberal leanings, a ruthless counter-campaign gradually took shape. In June 1986, the Republican Guard was responsible for killing 124 political prisoners in the aftermath of prison riots in Lima, while rumours of massacres of peasants in remote rural locations were rife. As always, democracy in Latin America could barely contain the violence in most countries.

The Football War

This was particularly apparent if one turned to events in Central America and the Caribbean, where the situation was exacerbated by the constant threat (and sometimes the reality) of superpower intervention. Levels of violence within parts of this region have always been high, with countries suffering both external and internal wars. In 1969, for example, hostilities broke out between Honduras and El Salvador, apparently over the results of football matches in a

"Baby Doc" Duvalier, accompanied by his wife, flees Haiti, 1986.

IDEOLOGICAL ARENA

Government troops fight the Sandinistas, Nicaragua, 1979.

qualifying round of the World Cup. On 8 June 1969 the Salvadorean team lost to Honduras in a match played at Tegucigalpa, the Honduran capital. A week later, the result was reversed in the second leg, played in San Salvador.

On both occasions, violence erupted, taking a nasty turn in Honduras when Salvadoreans who had settled in the country were singled out for attack. El Salvador declared a "state of emergency". On 27 June, the Salvadorean football team won the deciding match against Honduras in Mexico City, and this coincided with a breach in diplomatic relations between the two sides, followed closely by a Salvadorean invasion of Honduras.

By 18 July, when an OAS ceasefire came into force, Salvadorean troops had advanced approximately 24 km (15 miles); by August, when they finally withdrew, over 3,000 people (mainly civilians) had died in the fighting.

Nicaragua

By then, the situation in Central America had deteriorated dramatically, drawing the region to the forefront of the "New Cold War" between the superpowers. The confrontation began most noticeably in Nicaragua, where the authoritarian regime of Anastasio Somoza was overthrown by left-wing guerrillas in July 1979. Active opposition to the Somoza family dated back to 1958, when three former university students, Carlos Fonseca Amador, Silvio Mayorga and Tomas Borge, founded the FSLN (*Frente Sandinista de Liberación Nacional*), more commonly known as the Sandinistas.

Named after the legendary guerrilla leader of the 1920s and 1930s, Augusto Sandino, the new group began its operations in the northern mountains, gradually gaining popular support. In 1967 they tried to move from guerrilla to open warfare, gathering their forces at Mount Pancasan, but they were attacked and dispersed by Somoza's fiercely-loyal National Guard. For a time, it looked as if the threat had been effectively countered.

Sandinista revolution

The Sandinistas went underground and broadened their support among the middle classes alienated by Somoza's dictatorial rule. In December 1974 Sandinista guerrillas kidnapped a number of senior politicians and friends of the president, forcing him to pay a large ransom and to release 59 political prisoners. Somoza responded by taking a much more ruthless line, introducing repressive policies which did nothing to gain him popular support.

By 1977 the Sandinistas were carrying out open attacks on National Guard barracks and fomenting urban uprisings throughout the country. Two years later, as guerrilla columns closed in on the capital, Managua, Somoza fled to the United States. He was not to survive for long: in 1980 he was assassinated while on a visit to Paraguay.

Elections

Once the Sandinistas had gained power, they disbanded the National Guard (replacing it with a broader-based Sandinista People's Army) and introduced a variety of industrial, agrarian and educational reforms which showed the left-wing aspirations of the revolution.

Elections, monitored by outside bodies which declared them to be reasonably "free and fair", took place in October 1984. They confirmed President Daniel Ortega's Sandinista leadership, but by then the revolution had created a whole new set of problems. Opposition groups, known collectively as "Contras", had emerged, backed more or less openly by the United States.

The US reaction

In many ways, the US reaction was predictable, despite the clear parallels with the Cuban revolution. The success of the Sandinistas, like that of Castro in 1959, seemed to have caught the United States by surprise. It happened at a time when Jimmy Carter was more concerned about events in Iran. Yet, like Cuba, it threatened to undermine the United States' political, economic and strategic position in the Central American/Caribbean area.

In January 1981 Ronald Reagan came to office with the promise of taking a much firmer stand against the spread of communism worldwide. The United States accused Ortega of direct links with Castro (and, by implication, the Soviet Union).

To many of Reagan's supporters, the Sandinistas were little more than "puppets" of the politburo in Moscow, ready to exploit US weaknesses which had been allowed to develop under Carter. Chief among these was the fact that, in 1979, Carter had signed the Panama Canal Treaty, relinquishing US control of the Canal Zone to Panama and agreeing to the withdrawal of US bases (including the School of the Americas at Fort Gulick) from the region. With the communists already established in Cuba and Nicaragua, the threat to other countries in Central America and the Caribbean, including Panama, seemed very real indeed.

Grenada

The situation was made worse by events elsewhere in the area, for Nicaragua seemed to be merely the tip of the iceberg. In March 1979, for example, the left-wing New Jewel Movement had seized power in the small Caribbean island of Grenada (an ex-British colony, granted its independence in 1974). A People's Revolutionary Government was formed under Maurice Bishop and new social policies, not dissimilar to those of communism, were introduced.

The constitution was suspended, various civil liberties were curtailed and, most worrying of all to observers in Washington, Soviet and Cuban influence was obvious. The People's Revolutionary Army was being re-armed with Soviet weapons and a new airport at Point Salines, capable of taking long-range bombers, was being built under Cuban supervision. Again, parallels with Cuba were easy to make.

A youthful Sandinista, Managua, 1979.

El Salvador

A third area of crisis was El Salvador, the most densely populated and highly industrialised of the Central American republics. Despite success in the "Football War", a variety of factors had combined to produce, by the early 1980s, a bitter civil war. Inflation was running at 50 per cent a year and there was an unemployment rate of 40 per cent – rising to 70 per cent in some rural areas, where drought and a drop in world demand for coffee spelt economic disaster. Social discontent was deep-rooted, fuelling splits which already existed between the peasants and the ruling military élite.

Fraudulent elections in 1972 had led to the growth of armed opposition to the government, and by the end of the decade a familiar pattern of guerrilla attacks, assassinations and kidnaps had emerged. The Salvadorean Army, funded and equipped to a significant extent by the United States, had managed to suppress the worst of the trouble, although at high cost in terms of civil liberties – strikes were banned, public meetings broken up, agitators arrested (and tortured) and death squads allowed to flourish.

This led to a reassessment of support by the Carter administration in Washington, which made continued aid dependent on improvements in human rights. Suddenly, the *junta* faced new problems. In October 1979 a *coup d'état* ousted the existing government of General Carlos Humberto Romero Mena, bringing to power a coalition which included the more moderate politician José Napoleón Duarte.

Opposition groups

The violence continued, however, reaching fresh heights in 1980 when a right-wing death-squad gunned down the outspoken Archbishop of San Salvador, Oscar Romero, while he was conducting a religious service. This drove the various opposition groups to band together, forming the FDR (*Frente Democrático Revolucionario*) as a political "front", with the FMLN (*Farabundo Marti de Liberación Nacional*) as its military wing.

In 1981 the FMLN launched a major offensive which, although ultimately contained by the army, forced the ruling élite onto the defensive. In March 1982 yet more fraudulent elections ousted Duarte from power and led to the creation of a new government under extreme right-winger Major Roberto D'Aubuisson Arrieta.

He immediately reintroduced repressive counter-measures which did little to reduce the popular support

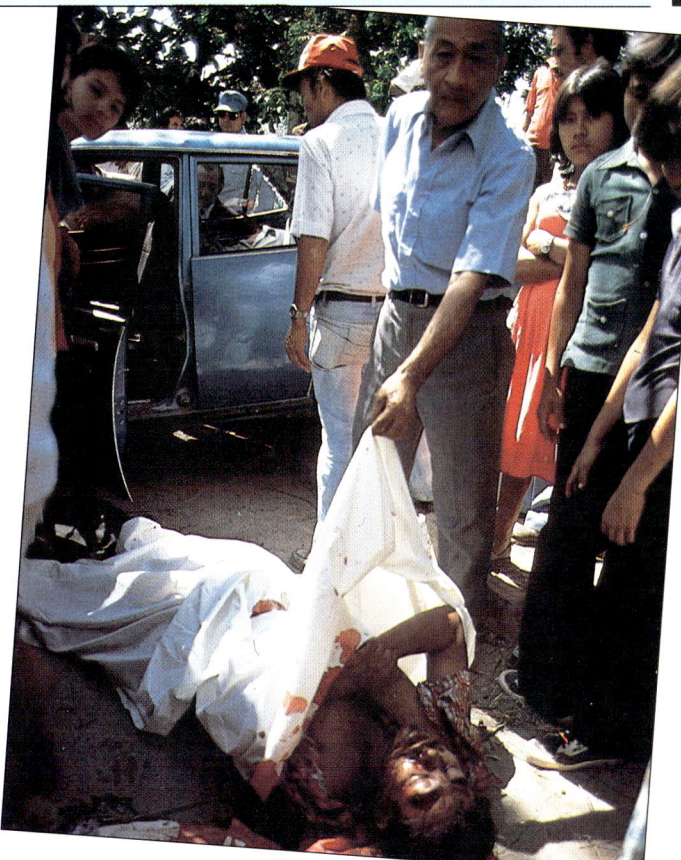

Violence in El Salvador: the killing goes on.

enjoyed by the FDR/FMLN and, as the violence continued, US pressure led to more elections in March 1984.

Duarte returned to power, dedicated to reform and direct negotiations with the rebels – something he was forced to do anyway in late 1985, when the FMLN kidnapped his daughter Ines – but by 1987 there seemed little prospect of an end to the fighting.

US fears of communism

To add to this, guerrilla movements continued to be active in Guatemala. Both Panama and Costa Rica were experiencing civil unrest, while Mexico faced a growing mountain of economic and social problems which left it vulnerable to political extremism. This meant the United States was becoming increasingly concerned about its "backyard".

The nightmare of communist expansion into Central America had moved one step closer to reality with events in Nicaragua. Elsewhere most of the weaknesses which, in the past, had opened the way to left-wing revolution were apparent. Carter had insisted on right-wing regimes respecting human rights as a condition for support. However, with the election of Reagan a much more sustained policy of anti-communism emerged.

CONFLICT IN THE 20TH CENTURY

THE CONTRAS IN NICARAGUA, 1984

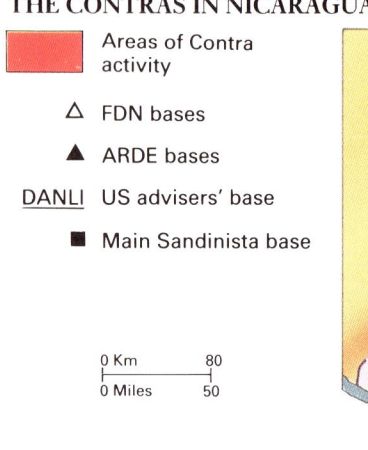

- ▨ Areas of Contra activity
- △ FDN bases
- ▲ ARDE bases
- DANLI US advisers' base
- ■ Main Sandinista base

Justifying US policy

The main problem facing the United States was one of consistency. Although it was understandable that Reagan should support the Duarte government against the FMLN in El Salvador, his simultaneous backing of the Contras – rebel groups fighting an elected Nicaraguan regime – was sometimes difficult to justify. This was particularly so to Western allies who did not fully appreciate the nature of the threat posed by communist expansion into Central America.

That threat was a very real one, however, and despite attempts by the US Congress to stop the funding of the Contras (a situation which contributed to the "Irangate" scandal of 1986-87, when it was discovered that money raised by the sale of arms to Iran was being diverted in secret to the Nicaraguan "freedom fighters"), the Reagan administration stuck to its policy of supporting anyone who opposed left-wing revolution. It was a policy which took a variety of forms.

At its most predictable level, US support was manifested in a steady flow of money, arms and military advisers to the anti-communist forces. As soon as Reagan came to office in 1981, CIA activity was increased among the Contras and "Green Beret" advisers began to appear on the ground, particularly in Honduras, where US bases were established.

By 1984, US reconnaissance aircraft flying out of Honduras were reporting on rebel movements in El Salvador, financial aid to both Duarte and the Contras was increasing and a special training centre for Salvadorean and Honduran army units had been set up. At the same time, a reported 1,500 US personnel were present in Honduras, with a further 100 in El Salvador as front-line advisers. Although the latter were meant to do no more than train the Salvadoreans in counter-insurgency techniques, the fact that they suffered casualties implied a more active role.

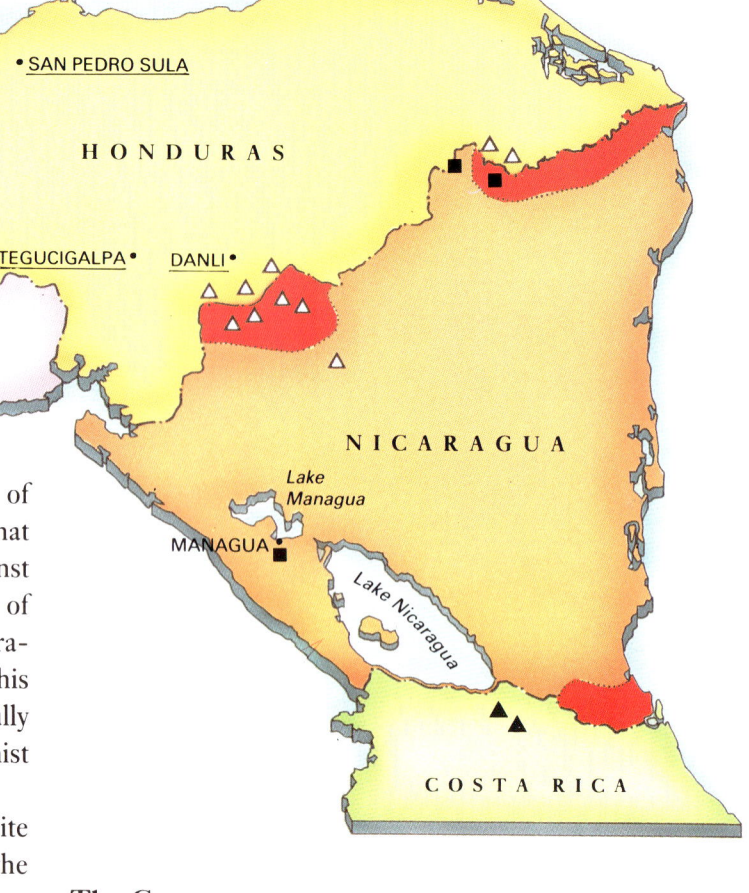

The Contras

There was little doubt that support of this nature was crucial to the success of Reagan's policy, but it was not always effective, as in the case of the Contras. Although they were supposed to constitute a solid bloc of opposition to the Sandinista regime, in reality they were hopelessly split.

The main group was the FDN (*Fuerzas Democráticas Nicaraguënses*), led by Adolfo Calero Portocarrero, drawing much of its support from ex-members of Somoza's National Guard and operating, with US backing, from bases in Honduras. But other groups also existed, notably the ARDE (*Alianza Revolucionaria Democrática*).

These groups invariably refused to co-operate, preferring to mount their own operations. In addition, the level of military skill was poor – in November 1985 for example, an FDN force which attacked a border town was dispersed and destroyed by a single Sandinista helicopter. There was also evidence that the Contras were killing innocent civilians in their raids. Indeed, the existence of the Contras gave the Sandinista leadership a threat with which to rally the Nicaraguan people and made them turn to the Cubans and Soviets for military aid.

The US invasion of Grenada

In such circumstances, the temptation to take more direct action, using the overwhelming power of the United States to prevent the spread of communism, was strong. A precedent was set in October 1983 when, in response to a deteriorating political situation in Grenada, Reagan authorised armed intervention at the invitation of the Organisation of Eastern Caribbean States. The members of this organisation were extremely worried and concerned about left-wing successes in their midst.

The crisis had come to a head on 19 October when Maurice Bishop, arrested a few days earlier by political rivals in the New Jewel Movement, was killed, along with some of his supporters who had tried to force his release. A new Revolutionary Military Council had been set up under Bernard Coard, and a 24-hour curfew imposed.

The US response was swift and effective. At 0536 hours on 25 October US Navy SEALs (Sea-Air-Land commando teams) secured Government House, close to the capital St George's, and prepared the way for a heliborne landing by US Marines at Pearls airport on the east coast of the island. Meanwhile, US Rangers attacked the unfinished airfield at Point Salines before advancing inland to the True Blue Medical School where a number of US students had taken shelter.

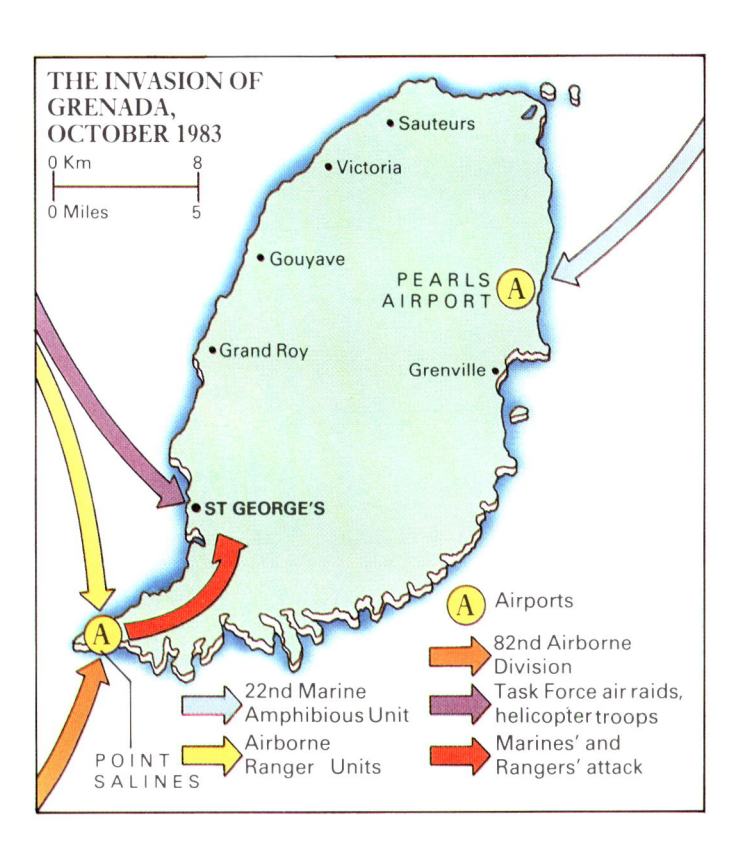

The invasion was completed at 0730 hours, when more Marines landed to the north of St George's, and by the afternoon of the 26th the fighting was over. Grenadiàn and Cuban resistance was stronger than anticipated, leading to the loss of 18 US servicemen, but the outcome was never really in doubt.

Further US intervention?

US forces withdrew from the island in November 1983, leaving just a few advisers to train a new defence force. Democratic elections, held in December, brought a more moderate government to power. Despite protests from a variety of sources worldwide, no one had rushed to Coard's aid, allowing the United States to carry out a short, sharp operation.

But this was a policy which could not be taken too far, for although the prospect of US intervention in Nicaragua could not be dismissed entirely, the chances of it succeeding without Soviet reaction and a possible superpower confrontation were small. Instead, Reagan had to be content with joint US-Honduran military exercises close to the Nicaraguan border.

These, together with a large US naval presence in the Caribbean, were probably designed to intimidate the Sandınıstas and force them to accept peace plans put forward by the Contadora Group of Latin American countries (Mexico, Panama, Colombia and Venezuela). If so, their record of success was poor, although this did not mean that peace proposals were always rejected. The so-called Arias Plan (named after President Arias of Costa Rica) for ceasefires in Nicaragua and El Salvador was signed on 7 August 1987 amid widely expressed hopes that regional stability would be re-established.

The future

By the late 1980s, therefore, few of the problems of Latin America had been resolved and violence was still endemic. Political stability was rare in countries with massive social and political divisions. Territorial disputes continued to cause conflict and outside influence in the region seemed to be increasing. In addition, poverty and social hardship were spreading.

In the absence of long-term solutions to these problems – solutions which can only come from a concerted global effort to release the region from its burden of debt and an equally concerted Latin American effort to use the considerable resources of the area to ensure social and economic improvement – the situation is unlikely to change.

CONFLICT IN THE 20TH CENTURY: APPENDICES

The countries of South and Central (Latin) America face a variety of problems. A tradition of government backed by military force has often led to dictatorship and repression, while revolutions, *coups d'état* and wars have kept violence at high levels. This, in turn, has fuelled inflation, leading to debt and deep poverty in some regions. Solutions are hard to find, although the recent trend towards democracy gives some hope for the future.

PERSONALITIES

Raúl Alfonsín (1926-) President of Argentina, 1983- . Born of a Spanish father and half-Welsh mother, Alfonsín attended a military academy before studying law at the University of La Plata. In 1963 he was elected a member of the Argentinian Chamber of Deputies, supporting the Radical Party. During the years of military rule and the "Dirty War", he remained quietly active in politics, assuming the leadership of the Radicals in June 1983. Four months later, he became President.

Jacobo Arbenz (1913-71) President of Guatemala, 1951-54. As a colonel, Arbenz took part in the revolt of 1944 in Guatemala, joining the revolutionary government as Minister of War. Appointed President in March 1951, he embarked on a programme of social and economic reforms which threatened US interests in the country (especially those of the United Fruit Company) and alarmed the government in Washington. He was overthrown when the CIA-backed forces of Colonel Carlos Castillo Armas invaded Guatemala (June 1954). He died in exile in Mexico in January 1971.

Jacobo Arbenz.

Fulgencio Batista (1901-73) President of Cuba, 1940-44; 1952-59. A soldier in the Cuban Army, Batista helped to organise the 1933 "Sergeants' Revolt". He became Chief of Staff of the Army which overthrew both President Carlos Manuel de Cespedes and his successor Ramón Grau San Martín. Elected President himself in 1940, Batista stepped down four years later, only to return to seize power again in 1952. Increasingly corrupt and repressive, he lost ground to Castro's rebels. Eventually he fled on 1 January 1959 as the *fidelistas* entered Havana.

Fidel Castro (1926-) Cuban revolutionary; leader of Cuba, 1959- . Educated as a lawyer, Castro first came to prominence in July 1953, when he led an attack on the Moncada Barracks. Imprisoned and then exiled, he returned to Cuba in December 1956 with a small group of rebels (*fidelistas*), intent on the overthrow of Batista. He started a guerrilla campaign and seized power in January 1959. He soon revealed his communist leanings. He survived both the Bay of Pigs (1961) and the Missile Crisis (1962) to become a firm supporter of Latin American revolution and a leading voice in Third World affairs.

Raúl Alfonsín.

Fulgencio Batista.

José Napoléon Duarte (1925-) President of El Salvador, 1984- . Educated at the University of Notre Dame, Indiana, Duarte entered politics in the early 1960s as a founder member of the Christian Democrat Party in El Salvador. Imprisoned and tortured by the military in 1972, he was forced into exile, only to return in 1979 as a member of a civilian-military *junta*. Elected President in June 1984, he faced the problem of balancing the power of the military against the mounting pressure from guerrillas.

François ("Papa Doc") Duvalier (1907-71) President of Haiti, 1957-71. After serving as Haitian Director of Public Health, 1944-48, and as Secretary of Labour, 1949-50, Duvalier was elected President in 1957. He maintained his authority by means of voodoo ("black magic") and repression, the latter carried out by the *Tontons Macoutes*. In 1964 he declared himself President for Life, ruling as an absolute despot until his death in 1971. He was succeeded by his son, Jean-Claude ("Baby Doc"), who ruled until February 1986.

Ernesto "Che" Guevara (1928-67) Argentinian-born revolutionary leader and guerrilla theorist. A trained doctor, Guevara was in Guatemala in 1954 when Jacobo Arbenz was overthrown by a CIA-backed invasion, and this confirmed his radical, anti-US beliefs. Joining Fidel Castro in Mexico in 1956, he became a successful guerrilla leader in the Cuban Revolt, entering Havana in late 1958. He served as Minister of Industry in Cuba, 1961-65, resigning to promote revolution in Latin America. He was killed leading a guerrilla campaign in Bolivia, October 1967.

Carlos Marighela (1909-69) Brazilian revolutionary and theorist of urban guerrilla warfare. Son of an Italian immigrant, Marighela joined the Brazilian Communist Party in 1925. After a few years at university, where he studied engineering, he dedicated his life to left-wing revolution. In October 1967, he broke with the communists to set up his own ALN (*Acção Libertadora Nacional*) and, in 1969, he produced *The Minimanual of Urban Guerrilla Warfare*. He was killed in a gun battle with police in November 1969.

Juan Domingo Perón (1895-1974) President of Argentina, 1946-55; 1973-74. An admirer of Italian fascism, Perón served as Secretary of Labour and Social Welfare, 1943-45. Arrested by the military, he was released after popular pressure and, in 1946, was elected President. His Vice-President – his wife Eva – died in 1952, after which Perón gradually lost his grip on power, being forced into exile in 1955. In 1973 the Perónist Party won the elections in Argentina and Perón resumed the presidency in October. He died in office, being succeeded by his wife, Isabelita.

Augusto Pinochet (1915-) President of Chile, 1974- . Educated at the Chilean Military Academy, Pinochet became a professional soldier, gradually rising through the officer ranks until promoted general in 1973. He led the *coup d'état* to overthrow President Salvador Allende in September 1973, becoming President himself a year later. Renowned for a ruthless use of power, he faced persistent opposition from left-wing guerrillas. By the mid-1980s, he was one of the few Latin American dictators still in office.

Anastasio Somoza (Junior) (1925-80) President of Nicaragua, 1967-72; 1974-79. Son of General Anastasio Somoza (President of Nicaragua, 1933-56) and brother of Luis Somoza (President, 1956-63), Anastasio Somoza (Junior) was educated in New York and at the US Military Academy, West Point. A member of the Nicaraguan National Guard since 1941, he rose to its command by 1967, when he was elected President of the country. He was overthrown by Sandinista guerrillas in 1979 and assassinated while on a visit to Paraguay a year later.

José Napoléon Duarte.

Augusto Pinochet.

Anastasio Somoza (Junior).

WAR AND REVOLUTION SINCE 1900

Latin America's reputation as a region of violence would appear to be well deserved. Although relatively unaffected by the two world wars of the 20th century, most of the countries of Latin America have suffered revolutions, civil wars or border/territorial clashes since 1900, some of which have led to widespread death and destruction.

The Mexican Revolution (1910-20)
Popular risings in October 1910, led by Emiliano Zapata in the south and Pancho Villa in the north, triggered revolts in the Federal Army and, in May 1911, forced the resignation of President Porfirio Díaz. He was replaced by Francisco Madero, but his hold on power was not secure: in February 1913 he was overthrown by General Victoriano Huerta who, in turn, was forced out of office in July 1914. The Federal Army collapsed and civil war ensued, fought between the "Constitutional Army" of Alvaro Obregón and the rebel forces led by Zapata and Villa. By November 1916, Villa's forces had collapsed. Following the death of Zapata in April 1919, Obregón's army gained the upper hand. Guerrilla warfare continued until July 1920, by which time over 50,000 military and civilian casualties had been reported.

The Chaco War (1932-35)
Bolivia, having lost its outlet to the sea during the Pacific War of 1879-83, sought to gain access to the upper Paraguay river by laying claim to the Chaco region between Bolivia and Paraguay. Minor clashes between the armies of the two countries began in 1927, leading to all-out war in 1932. The Paraguayans advanced into Bolivia, only to suffer a setback in November 1932 which led to stalemate; a second Paraguayan offensive in September 1933 had much the same effect. Fighting continued, but by June 1935 both sides were close to exhaustion. Hostilities ended on 14 June, by which time the Paraguayans had lost an estimated 36,000 men and the Bolivians 57,000. A peace treaty in July 1938 confirmed Paraguayan claims to the Chaco region.

The Ecuador-Peru War (1941)
In July 1941, Peru invaded southern Ecuador, advancing rapidly to seize vast tracts of disputed border territory. Hostilities lasted only three weeks, during which the superior Peruvian forces overwhelmed those of Ecuador with relative ease. A peace treaty, signed in January 1942, transferred most of the disputed ground to Peru.

Soviet-built Hind helicopters of the Sandinista government, Nicaragua, 1987.

British commandos practise helicopter drill, Falklands War, 1982.

The Colombian Civil War (1948-57)
The murder of left-wing leader Jorge Eliécer Gaitán in April 1948 led to an explosion of violence in the capital, Bogotá, which rapidly spread to the rest of the country. Remembered as *La Violencia*, the bloodletting continued for almost a decade as Conservative and Liberal factions fought for political advantage. By 1957 the country was close to collapse, having lost over 200,000 of its people. A return to democracy, confirmed by elections in March 1958, ended the fighting.

The Cuban Revolution (1956-59).
On 2 December 1956, Fidel Castro and 81 armed followers landed in Cuba, intent on the overthrow of President Fulgencio Batista. Using the hills of the Sierra Maestra as a base and gaining support from the urban-based 26th July Movement, the *fidelistas* gradually increased the pressure through guerrilla action. As Batista became more and more isolated, guerrilla columns, led by Camilo Cienfuegos and Che Guevara, advanced on Havana. Batista fled on 1 January 1959.

The Nicaraguan Revolution and Civil War (1962-   )
Although created in 1958, the *Frente Sandinista de Liberación Nacional* (FSLN) did not begin its campaign of guerrilla violence against the existing regime until the early 1960s. At first, its impact was small, but after a massacre of demonstrators by the National Guard in January 1967, popular support began to grow. Guerrilla attacks, backed by protests and demonstrations, gradually undermined the regime of Anastasio Somoza (Junior) until, in July 1979, he was forced to flee. Almost immediately, however, National Guardsmen loyal to Somoza regrouped in Honduras and began their own guerrilla campaign against the new Sandinista government. Supported by the United States, "Contra" groups such as the *Fuerzas Democráticas Nicaragüenses* (FDN) and the *Alianza Revolucionaria Democrática* (ARDE) mounted cross-border raids into Nicaragua, although their impact was undermined by internal rifts. By 1987 there were a few signs of an end to the fighting.

The "Football War" (1969)
The movement of illegal immigrants from El Salvador into Honduras led to strained relations between the two countries, and these were made worse as their football teams met in a qualifying round of the World Cup in 1969. On 14 July, Salvadorean forces crossed the border into Honduras, advancing along the Pan-American Highway. An OAS ceasefire was imposed in early August, by which time over 3,000 people (mainly civilians) had been killed.

The Falklands War (1982)
In early 1982, the Argentinian ruling *junta*, led by General Leopoldo Galtieri, decided to resolve the long-running dispute with Britain over the Falklands (Malvinas) by force. On 2 April, Argentinian forces occupied the islands and, 24 hours later, seized the dependency of South Georgia. The British responded with diplomatic and economic measures, backed by a naval task force and the declaration of an "exclusion zone" around the islands. South Georgia was recaptured in late April and, a month later, British forces landed on East Falkland. Argentinian air attacks inflicted significant damage on British shipping, but this was not enough to prevent a British advance on the Falklands capital, Port Stanley. Battles at Goose Green (27/28 May) and among the hills overlooking Port Stanley (11-14 June) led to an Argentinian surrender on 14 June.

MAJOR GUERRILLA GROUPS

The successful seizure of power by Fidel Castro in Cuba in 1959 led to a spate of predominantly left-wing insurgencies throughout Latin America. To begin with, the groups involved tried to follow the Cuban model, but by the late 1960s the advantages of rural-based operations had been largely negated by strong government action.

A shift to the cities then took place, producing the phenomenon of urban guerrilla warfare which, in many cases, degenerated into terrorism. This, in turn, triggered harsh government counter-measures which few groups proved able to withstand and, by the late 1970s, the insurgent threat seemed to have subsided. The success of the Sandinistas in Nicaragua in 1979, however, provided a new model which, by the mid-1980s, had still to be discredited.

Argentina
Montoneros: active in the early 1970s as a militant wing of the Perónist movement, the group first came to prominence in May 1970 when its members kidnapped (and subsequently killed) ex-President Pedro Aramburu. Dedicated to achieving the return to power of Juan Perón, the Montoneros seemed to have succeeded when he was re-elected President in late 1973, but by then their demands had become too left-wing to be acceptable. Denounced by Perón in 1974, the group reverted to a campaign of violence. From 1975-76 street fighting was at its height and the Argentinian military seized power in March 1976. They cracked down hard on insurgents during the "Dirty War", during which 15,000 are thought to have died. By 1981, the Montoneros no longer existed.

Brazil
Acção Libertadora Nacional (ALN): formed by Carlos Marighela in October 1967 when he broke with the Brazilian Communist Party. Responsible for the kidnap of US Ambassador Charles Burke Elbrick in September 1969, the group did not survive the death of Marighela two months later. By 1970, most of its activists were dead, in prison or in exile.

Colombia
Ejército de Liberación Nacional (ELN): formed in July 1964 on the Cuban model, the group suffered internal splits two years later and, under increasing pressure from government forces, gradually lost its leaders and its impact. Reports of ELN activity still appeared in the 1980s, but it was no longer a force to be reckoned with.

French nuns, kidnapped by Montoneros guerrillas, Argentina, 1977.

APPENDICES

A young guerrilla of the FMLN, El Salvador, 1987.

El Salvador
Farabundo Marti de Liberación Nacional (FMLN): created in 1980 as the military wing of the *Frente Democrático Revolucionario* (FDR), itself a political "front" for a wide variety of opposition groups. Named after the communist leader Farabundo Marti (killed in 1932), the FMLN had its origins in an earlier insurgent group, the *Fuerzas Populares de Liberación* (FPL), which had been active since 1977. By the mid-1980s, the FMLN was exerting considerable pressure on the elected government of José Napoleón Duarte.

Guatemala
Fuerzas Armadas Rebeldes (FAR): formed in 1962 by left-wing army officers, the group was responsible for a number of spectacular kidnaps in the mid-1960s. After the failure of its 1962 attempt to raise the countryside in revolt, it moved to the cities, but it never gained popular support. It suffered badly at the hands of US-trained government forces, however, and by 1967 had been forced into an alliance with the *Movimiento Revolucionario 13 de Noviembre* (MR-13). Although still active in the 1980s, the threat posed by the group was not large.

Nicaragua
Frente Sandinista de Liberación Nacional (FSLN or Sandinistas): named after the Nicaraguan patriot Augusto Sandino (killed by government forces in 1934), the group was set up in 1958 by Carlos Fonseca Amador, dedicated to the overthrow of the Somoza regime. Of little consequence until the mid-1970s, when they carried out a number of successful kidnaps, the Sandinistas gradually gained support as Anastasio Somoza (Junior) lost popularity. In July 1979, the rebels took over power – the first successful insurgency in Latin America since 1959.

Peru
Sendero Luminoso (SL or "Shining Path"): created in 1970 by Abimael Guzmán from a splinter group within the Peruvian Communist Party. More concerned with philosophy than action, the SL did not turn to violence until 1980, drawing its support from the rural Indian population with its long tradition of resentment. By the mid-1980s, the SL had built up a reputation for carrying out both rural and urban operations, imposing mounting pressure on the elected government of Peru under Alan García.

Uruguay
Movimiento de Liberación Nacional (MLN or Tupamaros): founded in the early 1960s by Raúl Sendic, the group had its origins in rural trade unions, particularly among the sugar workers. Selected guerrilla attacks were carried out in the mid-1960s but, when these failed to have any effect on the government, Sendic shifted his campaign to Montevideo. Between 1968 and 1973, the Tupamaros constituted a major threat, disclosing evidence of government corruption, kidnapping foreign representatives (notably US AID official Dan Mitrione in 1970 and British Ambassador Geoffrey Jackson a year later) and stealing money to give to the poor. The government response – allowing the military to conduct a "no-holds-barred" counter-insurgency campaign – led to the destruction of the Tupamaros.

Venezuela
Movimiento de Izquierda Revolucionaria (MIR): founded in 1960 as a "copy" of Castro's movement in Cuba. Initially linked to the Venezuelan Communist Party, a major split within the MIR in 1968 weakened its impact. After a short campaign of bank robberies and kidnaps, the group folded in the early 1970s. An allied group under Douglas Bravo – the *Fuerzas Armadas de Liberación Nacional* (FALN) – fared little better.

DEBT

In August 1982, the Mexican government announced that it had run out of money and that it could no longer afford to pay the interest on its huge international loans, raised through the World Bank. Other Latin American countries, notably Argentina, Brazil and Venezuela, predicted that they would soon be in a similar situation, creating a "debt crisis" which threatened the Western world and its banking system.

Borrowing money

The system of international lending is not complicated. Any country in need of money to help develop its economy – by opening up new areas of mineral exploitation or building new industries – can approach the World Bank. This was set up by the United Nations in the 1940s to provide appropriate funds. As the countries of the communist bloc regard this as an instrument of Western capitalism, they will not make any contributions, but there are enough banks and financial institutions in the West (particularly the United States) to ensure a steady flow of money.

In addition, since the early 1970s, the enormous amounts of "petrodollars" (money raised by the sale of oil, especially in the Middle East) have boosted investment funds. These are co-ordinated through the International Monetary Fund (IMF) and the cash offered to the country in need, with interest rates laid down according to the projected ability of that country to "service" or pay off its debts. If the process works smoothly, the wealth created by the new mineral or industrial projects should ensure economic growth which, in turn, will enable repayments to be made on time.

Economic problems

Unfortunately for both lender and debtor, this has rarely happened in the case of Latin America. One of the weaknesses of the system is that it takes no account of international or domestic political and economic factors which may affect a country's ability to repay its debts. Thus, for example, the Western banks were more than willing to lend enormous sums to oil-producing countries such as Venezuela or Mexico in the aftermath of the oil-price boom in the early 1970s. They little realised that over-production in the Middle East, coupled with a policy of stockpiling by Western countries determined to avoid the effects of an embargo by Middle East oil-producers, would lead to a "glut" and, by the mid-1980s, a drop in the price of oil. Similarly, money was lent to Brazil in the early 1970s for the construction of the Pan-Amazonian Highway. However the project was over-ambitious and its costs increased at an alarming rate.

When, in addition, the commodity market for minerals such as tin and copper virtually collapsed in the 1980s, any hopes of wealth from new areas of exploitation soon disappeared. High interest rates on existing loans and the emergence of a strong US dollar did little to help. As loans are repaid in US dollars, some countries were having to spend more of their own currency just to produce the necessary repayments.

The Pan-Amazonian highway was an expensive project started in the 1970s.

Uncontrolled borrowing

By then, however, it was too late to reverse the trend of unlimited lending, and the figures speak for themselves. In 1970, Latin America as a whole owed a manageable $20 billion to the IMF; by 1980 that figure had risen to $160 billion and, by 1986, had rocketed to a distinctly unmanageable $360 billion. Indeed, in some countries such as Argentina, Mexico and Brazil, most of the money raised from the sale of exports was needed just to repay the interest on existing loans, leaving virtually nothing to stimulate economic growth. A crisis was inevitable.

Inflation and unrest

The results were dramatic. Domestically the need to find money for loan repayment often led to a suspension or cancellation of the very projects which occasioned the debt in the first place. The inevitable result was that people lost their jobs. At the same time, as money became less readily available, inflation increased, reaching astronomical heights in some countries.

In 1985, for example, Argentina was suffering an annual inflation rate of 387 per cent while Bolivia, facing the collapse of the international tin market, reached an unbelievable 11,300 per cent! When this happened, it was the poor who suffered most, lacking the means to cushion themselves against the sudden drop in the value of money. At the same time, population growth showed no signs of declining. Conditions in the "shanty towns" which already existed around many Latin American cities deteriorated, and social problems of deprivation increased, leading to resentment and a potential for violence. Natural disasters such as the Mexican earthquake of 1985 merely made matters worse.

Solutions

Finding solutions has not been easy. Some Latin American countries have tried to help themselves by introducing stringent economic reforms, imposing wage restraint, combatting corruption and channelling available funds into less ambitious, short-term mineral or industrial projects. Some success has been achieved – in Argentina, for example, policies introduced by Raúl Alfonsín since 1983 have enabled him to cut inflation and to restart loan repayments on a regular basis – but the social pressures involved can lead to domestic trouble.

Another approach has been tried by the so-called Cartagena Group of Latin American countries (Argentina, Bolivia, Brazil, Chile, Colombia, the Dominican Republic, Ecuador, Mexico, Peru, Uruguay and Venezuela). This group has called for a rearrangement of existing loans to make repayment more manageable. At the same time, the United States, aware of the consequences of the "debt crisis" on Western banks, introduced more favourable loan facilities through the Baker Plan (named after Treasury Secretary James Baker) in 1985.

These are sensible moves which have defused the crisis in the short term. But more permanent solutions will require an acceptance by the Western banks that future loans must be made more flexible and less geared to the idea of profit for the lender. That is unlikely to happen overnight.

Part of a "shanty town" in Guyaquil, Ecuador.

THE DRUGS CONNECTION

The manufacture and sale of illegal drugs is a multi-billion dollar business in the modern world. A steady increase in demand from desperate addicts, particularly in the United States and Western Europe, guarantees a market, while the enormous size of the drugs trade and its close association with organised crime syndicates make it virtually impossible to police. To many observers, it is the most serious social problem currently facing the West.

Cocaine and crack

One of the most harmful drugs is cocaine and its highly addictive derivative known as "crack". Both are by-products of the coca plant, the leaves of which are ground down into a rough paste before being refined into snow-white cocaine powder. Further treatment with selected chemicals leads to the formation of crystals and crack.

The unrefined leaves of the coca plant are chewed as a source of fairly harmless food. However the vast majority of coca plants are grown to satisfy the needs of cocaine addicts. As over 90 per cent of the world's coca plants grow in Bolivia and Peru, South America is a major link in the drugs chain.

Producing coca leaves

The reasons for this are not difficult to understand. Coca has for long been a source of food among the Indians of the Andes and the plant is well suited to the soil and weather of the region. It is also easy to cultivate, requiring little attention yet producing its first crop of leaves within six months of planting. Thereafter, leaves may be picked up to six times a year, creating a steady source of income at very little outlay in terms of money.

But there is more to it than that, for in many cases the coca crop is all that stands between the farmer and starvation, particularly in countries suffering from inflation or the failure of other sources of peasant income. In Bolivia, for example, the collapse of the world tin market in the early 1980s left many peasants without jobs, money or prospects, tempting them into drugs production merely to survive. As they produce a commodity – coca leaves – which is not strictly illegal and as, in the vast majority of cases, they receive very small amounts of money (in relation to profits later in the chain), the peasants' role is hardly a deliberately evil one.

The drug barons

It is what happens to the coca once it has left the farmers' hands that is important, for it is here that the real profits are made. Some of the coca may be refined on the spot in illicit jungle laboratories, but the majority is shipped (illegally) to Colombia, a country which, it is estimated, produces more than 75 per cent of the world's cocaine, earning up to $5 billion a year in the process.

The trade is rarely sanctioned by the government or its officials (although a proportion of such officials must be corrupt enough to turn a blind eye when it is necessary), and the money ends up in private rather than public hands, but the traffic is often so deeply rooted that any attempts to stop it would lead to widespread violence.

Indeed, it is not unknown for governments to be deeply implicated in the trade – in Bolivia, for example, General Garcia Meza, who seized power in 1980, was widely suspected of being supported and funded by the country's cocaine "barons". In Colombia, the drug barons were powerful enough to arrange the murder of Chief Justice Minister Rodrigo Lara Bonilla in 1984. They escaped detection because they had paid off judges and police.

Coca leaves laid out to dry, Colombia.

Shifting the trade

All of this makes counter-measures extremely difficult to put into effect, yet it is essential that they be tried if the problem of drugs abuse is not to spread. Western countries try to prevent importing the drugs by searching suspect shipping or stopping smugglers as they try to enter. However with cocaine and crack coming by many different routes into the United States and Western Europe and the smugglers employing ever more sophisticated methods, customs officials are often overwhelmed by the sheer scale of the problem.

In such circumstances, a logical answer is to go to the root of the trade, destroying the coca plants before they can be refined. One way of doing this would be to offer an alternative source of income to the peasants of Peru or Bolivia, but this poses a number of problems. Their poverty and deprivation invariably arises from the economic situation in their countries. In order to improve this, reform of the world economic order is essential, at least to the extent where poorer countries can receive fairer and more flexible loans. Even then, there are no guarantees that money would be used to alleviate peasant problems. In too many cases, the Indians are last on the list when it comes to government aid.

That leaves very little alternative except military action, sending troops into remote jungle areas to destroy the coca crops and dismantle the illicit laboratories. In 1985, recognising the scale of the drugs problem, the United States offered to provide appropriate forces to carry out this task and the Bolivians agreed to the deployment of US helicopters and soldiers. They carried out a series of raids deep into jungle areas. Within days, the crops had been replanted and the laboratories rebuilt.

A long-term solution

As a symbol of US concern, the raids were important, but they were attacking the symptoms rather than the cause of increased coca production. The fight to halt the flow of cocaine and crack has to be more wide-ranging than that, going to the very roots of Latin America's problems. Until economic reforms on a global scale have been introduced, it is unrealistic to expect the starving farmers of South America to cease production of a crop which allows them to survive.

An illicit cocaine laboratory deep in the Bolivian jungle.

CHRONOLOGY

1945
February Chapultepec Meeting of American Republics

October Getúlio Vargas resigns as President of Brazil

1946
February Juan Perón elected President of Argentina

1947
September Inter-American Treaty of Reciprocal Assistance (Rio Treaty) signed

1948
January Organisation of American States (OAS) set up

April Civil war in Colombia (*La Violencia*) begins (lasts until 1957)

April Civil war in Costa Rica; democracy established and army disbanded

1950
May General Paul Magloire assumes power in Haiti in aftermath of a military coup

October Getúlio Vargas re-elected President of Brazil

November President Carlos Chalbaud of Venezuela assassinated

1951
March Colonel Jacobo Arbenz appointed President of Guatemala

May President Arias of Panama deposed by popular revolt

1952
March Fulgencio Batista seizes power in Cuba

April Popular rising in Bolivia overthrows military government

December Jiménez retakes power in Venezuela

1953
June General Gustavo Rojas Pinilla seizes power in Colombia

July Rebel assault on Moncada Barracks, Cuba; Fidel Castro captured and imprisoned (released, 1955)

1954
May General Alfredo Stroessner seizes power in Paraguay

June CIA-backed invasion of Guatemala; President Jacobo Arbenz overthrown

August Getúlio Vargas, President of Brazil, commits suicide

1955
January President José Remón of Panama assassinated

September Perón resigns as President of Argentina

1956
September Anastasio Somoza (Senior), President of Nicaragua, assassinated; succeeded by his son, Luis

December Fidel Castro lands in Cuba with 81 followers

December President Magloire flees from Haiti

1957
May Military coup deposes President Pinilla of Colombia

September Dr François ("Papa Doc") Duvalier elected President of Haiti

1958
January President Jiménez of Venezuela deposed in popular revolt

December *Fidelista* rebels enter Havana (Cuba)

1959
January President Batista flees from Cuba; Castro seizes power

1961
April CIA-backed Cuban exiles defeated at Bay of Pigs by Castro

May General Rafael Trujillo Molina, ruler of the Dominican Republic since 1930, assassinated

August President John F Kennedy of the United States initiates the "Alliance for Progress"

1962
July General Perez Godoy seizes power in Peru

October Cuban Missile Crisis

1963
March President Godoy of Peru deposed; replaced by Belaúnde Terry

September Military coup deposes President Juan Bosch of the Dominican Republic

1964

April General Humberto Castelo Branco seizes power in Brazil

November General René Barrientos Ortuño seizes power in Bolivia, starting a series of coups which continue until 1982

1965

April US intervention in the Dominican Republic

1967

October Death of Che Guevara in Bolivia

1968

October Arias regains power in Panama; deposed by General Omar Torrijos Herrera after only 11 days

October General Velasco Alvarado seizes power in Peru

1969

July-August "Football War" between Honduras and El Salvador

November Death of Carlos Marighela in Brazil

1971

April "Papa Doc" Duvalier of Haiti dies, succeeded by his son, Jean-Claude ("Baby Doc")

1972

February General Guillermo Rodríguez Lara seizes power in Ecuador

April State of "Internal War" in Uruguay against Tupamaros

1973

February Military assume predominant role in government of Uruguay

September Salvador Allende, Marxist President of Chile, deposed in a coup led by General Augusto Pinochet

October Juan Perón re-elected President of Argentina

1974

July Death of Juan Perón; his wife Isabelita assumes the presidency of Argentina

1975

April Military coup in Honduras brings Colonel Melgar Castro to power

August President Velasco Alvarado of Peru overthrown in a military coup

1976

January President Rodríguez Lara of Ecuador deposed in military coup

March Isabelita Perón of Argentina deposed by General Jorge Rafael Videla

June Military take over complete power in Uruguay

1979

April Restoration of elective government in Ecuador

July President Anastasio Somoza (Junior) of Nicaragua overthrown by Sandinista guerrillas

October Panama Canal Treaty

October President Carlos Humberto Romero of El Salvador deposed by civilian-military *junta*

1982

March Major Roberto D'Aubuisson Arrieta elected President of El Salvador

March General Efraín Rios Montt seizes power in Guatemala

April-June Falklands War between Britain and Argentina

October Elected government established in Bolivia

1983

August President Rios Montt of Guatemala deposed in a military coup

October Raúl Alfonsín elected President of Argentina

October US invasion of Grenada

1984

March José Napoleón Duarte elected President of El Salvador

October Beagle Channel Treaty between Argentina and Chile

October Elections in Nicaragua; Daniel Ortega of the Sandinistas becomes President

November Elections in Uruguay bring Julio Sanguinetti to power

1986

February "Baby Doc" Duvalier flees from Haiti

1987

August Central American republics agree to regional peace plan put forward by President Oscar Arias of Costa Rica

INDEX

Note: Numbers in bold refer to illustrations or maps

AAA (*Alianza Anticommunista Argentina*), 37
Admiral Graf Spee, 16, **16**, 17
Alabama National Guard, 27
Alfonsín, Raúl, 41, 48, **48**, 55
Allende, Salvador, 35, 49
Alliance for Progress, 31
ALN (*Acção Libertadora Nacional*), 34, 49, 52
Amador, Carlos Fonseca, 43, 53
Amazon river, 13
American Revolution, 8, 10
Anaya, Admiral Jorge, 38
Aramburu, General Pedro Eugenio, 19, 52
Arana, Major Francisco Javier, 22
Arbenz Guzman, Captain Jacobo, 22, 30, 48, **48**, 49
ARDE (*Alianza Revolucionaria Democrática*), 46, 51
Arévalo, Juan José, 22
Argentina, 8, 10, 12, 17, 48, 54, 55; Perónismo, 19-20, 36-37, **36**, **49**; Dirty War, 37-38, **37**, **38**, 41, 48, 52, **52**; Falklands War, 38-42, **40**, 51, **51**
Argentinian Air Force, 39-41
Argentinian Navy, 39-41
Arias, General, 47
Arias Plan, 47
Armas, Colonel Carlos Castillo, 48
Atlantic Conveyor, 40
Axis powers, 17
Aztecs, 7

B-26 Bombers, 27
Bahamas, 7
Baker Plan, 55
Baker, Secretary James, 55
Balaguer, Dr Joaquin, 32
Barrientos, Rene, 30-31
Batista, Fulgencio, 20, 22-25, **25**, 29, 31, 48, **48**
Bay of Pigs invasion, 27-28, **28**, 29, 48
Beagle Channel, 41
Beagle Channel Treaty, 41
Belgrano, see *General Belgrano*
Belize, 8
Betancourt, Romulo, 30
Bishop, Maurice, 44, 47
Bissell, Richard, 27
Blanco, Hugo, 29
Bogotá, 17

Bolivár, Simon, 8, **8**, 9
Bolivia, 8, 9, 12, 13, **13**, 17, 21, **21**, 30-31, **31**, 50, 55, 56-57
Bolivian Army, 30-31
Bordaberry, Juan María, 35
border disputes, 12-13, **13**
Borge, Tomas, 43
Bosch, Juan, 32
Bravo, Douglas, 53
Brazil, **7**, 8, 9, 12, 17, 20, **20**, 32, 34, 35, 36, 37, 42, 49, 52, 54, **54**, 55
Brazilian Expeditionary Force, 17
Brigade 2506, 28, **28**
Britain: 33, 44; colonial empire, 8; Second World War, 16-17; Falklands War, 38-41, 51, **51**
Buenos Aires, 9, 10, 38, **38**, 39, 41

Caamano, Francisco, 32
California, 8, 13
Campora, Dr Hector, 37
Canal Zone, see Panama Canal
Cape Horn, 7, 27
Cárdenas, Lázaro, 21
Carías, General Tiburcio, 21
Caribbean islands: colonial empires, 7, 8; US intervention, 14, 27-29, 44-47; Second World War, 17; communism, 24, 27-29, 44-47
Carlos III, 8
Carlos IV, 8
Carranza, Venustiano, 11
Carrera, Rafael, 12
Cartagena Group, 55
Carter, Jimmy, 38, 44, 45
Castro, Fidel, 23-24, **23**, 26, 28, 29, 30, 31, 32, 44, 48, 49, 52, 53
Catholic Church, 10, 19, 31, 41
caudillos, 10-11, 21, 42
CCC (*Comando Caça Communista*), 34
Central American Confederation, 11, 12
Central Intelligence Agency (CIA), 22, 27, 35, 48, 49
centralists, 10, 12
Cespedes, President Carlos Manuel de, 48
Chaco War, 13, **13**, 50
Chapultepec, 17
Chile, 7, 8, 9, 12, 17, 18, **34**, 35, **35**, 41, 42, 49, 55
China, 22, 29
Cienfuegos, Major Camilo, 24
Coard, Bernard, 47
cocaine, 56-57
coca plant, 56-57, **56**, **57**
coffee, **7**
Cold War, 22-25, 26-27
Colombia, 8, 12, 13, 14-15, 17, 21, 29, 47, 51, 52, 55, 56-57
Colombian Civil War, 21, 51

Columbus, Christopher, 7
Commando Brigade, 3rd, 39, 40
communism and communist movements, 17, 18, 22-25, 26-35, 44-47
conquistadores, 7
Constitutional Army, 50
Contadora Group, 47
"Contras", 44, 46-47, 51
Cordoba, 36, **37**
Cortés, Hernan, 7
Costa Rica, 11, 21, 32, 45, 47
counter-insurgency (COIN) techniques, 31, 46
coups d'état, 10, 11, 18, 20, 21
crack, 56-57
creoles, 8, 9, 10
Cuba, 7, 14, 17, 20, 48; revolution, 22-25, **23**, **25**, 44; and Cold War, 26, 28, **28**, 29, **29**, 30, 31, 32, 46, 47, 52, 53
Cuban blockade, 28, 29
Cuban exiles, 27, 28
Cuban Missile Crisis, 28, **29**, 48

Darwin, 40
D'Aubuisson Arrieta, Major Roberto, 45
death squads, 34, 37, 45
debt crisis, 54-55
debts, 7, 13, 54-55
Díaz, Porfirio, 11, 50
Dirty War, 37-38, **38**, 41, 48, 52
Dominican Republic, 7, 12, 15, 20, 32, **32**, 55
Dozo, Brigadier Basilio Lami, 38
drugs and drugs trade, 56-57, **56**, **57**
Duarte, Iñes, 45
Duarte, José Napoléon, 45, 46, 49, **49**, 53
Duvalier, Jean-Claude "Baby Doc", 42, 49
Duvalier, Dr François "Papa Doc", see Papa Doc

East Falkland, 40, 51
Ecuador, 8, 10, 12, 13, **13**, 17, 50, 55, **55**
Ecuador-Peru War, 12, 50
Eisenhower, Dwight D, 26, 27
Elbrick, Charles Burke, 34, 52
ELN (*Ejército de Liberación Nacional*), 29, 52
El Salvador, 10, 12, 20, 42-43, 45, **45**, 46, 47, 49, 51, 53, **53**
ERP (*Ejército Revolucionario del Pueblo*), 36-37, 38, 42
Exocet sea-skimming missiles, 40

Falkland Islands, 38-41, **40**, 41, 51, **51**
FALN (*Fuerzas Armadas de Liberación Nacional*), 53

FAR (*Fuerzas Armadas Rebeldes*), 30, 53
FARC (*Fuerzas Armadas Revolucionarias Colombianas*), 29
fascism, 17, 19
FDN (*Fuerzas Democráticas Nicaragüenses*), 46, 51
FDR (*Frente Democrático Revolucionario*), 45, 53
federalists, 9, 10
fidelistas, 24, 29, 48
FIR (*Frente de Izquierda Revolucionaria*), 29
FMLN (*Farabundo Marti de Liberación Nacional*), 45, 46, 53, **53**
foco theory, 29, 30, 31
Football War, 42-43, 45, 51
FPL (*Fuerzas Populares de Liberación*), 53
France, 3; colonial empires, 8; and Mexico, 13-14; Second World War, 17
French Revolution, 8, 10
FSLN (*Frente Sandinista de Liberación Nacional*), see Sandinistas

Gaitan, Eliecer, 51
Galtieri, Leopoldo, 38-41, **39**, 41, 51
García, Alan, 42, 53
gauchos, 10
General Belgrano, 40
Godoy, Hector Garcia, 32
gold, 7-8
Good Neighbour scheme, 15
Goulart, Joao, 34
Granma, 23
Great Depression, 12, 15
Grenada, 44, 47
Grupo de Oficiales Unidos, 19
Guantanamo, 14
Guatemala, 10, 12, 22, 26, 27, 30, 45, 48, 53
Guatemala City, 22
Guatemalan Communist Party, 22
guerrillas and guerrilla wars 26-35, 36-37, 42-43, 45-47, 52-53
guerrilla strategy, 28-29, 31, 32-33, 34
Guevara, Ernesto "Che", 24, 29, 30-31, **31**, 49
Guzmán, Abimael, 53

Haiti, 7, 12, 15, 20, 29, 35, 42, **42**, 49
Harriet, 40
Havana, 14, 17, 24, 28, 29, 30, 48
Hispaniola, see Haiti *and* Dominican Republic
Honduras, 11, 12, 20-21, 22, 32, 42-43, 46, 51
Huerta, General Victoriano, 50

INDEX

Incas, 7
inflation, 55
Inter-American Peace Force, 32
Inter-American Treaty of Reciprocal Assistance, see Rio Treaty
International Monetary Fund (IMF), 54, 55
Intrepid, HMS, 39
Irangate, 46

Jackson, Geoffrey, 35, 53
Jiménez, Colonel Marcos Pérez, 20
Johnson, Lyndon B, 32
Joseph I, 8
Juárez, Benito, 14
July Movement, 26th, 23-24, 29
Justicialismo, 19, 36
Justicialista (Perónist) Party, 37
Justo, Agustin, 19

Kennedy, John F, 27-28, 31
Khrushchev, Nikita, 28, 31
Korean War, 17, 22

Lamarca, Carlos, 34
landownership and land reform, 8, 10, 11, 30, 12, 19, 33
La Violencia, 21, 51
Latin America, colonial empires, 6-8; independence, 8-10; forms of government, 10-11; economy, 12, 18, 27, 33, 35, 45, 54-55; local wars, 12-14, 50-51; role of United States, 14-15, 22-25, 26-28, 31-32, 34-35, 38, 39, 44-47; World War II, 16-17; role of army and military rule, 18, 19, 20, 29, 34, 35, 38-39, 41, 42; reform, 19, 20, 22, 24; communist movements, 21-22, 24, 44-47; guerrilla movements, 21, 26-35, 36-37, 42-43, 44, 52-53, **52, 53**; drugs and drug trade, 56-57, **56, 57**
Lonardi, Eduardo, 19

Madero, Francisco, 11, 50
Maine, USS, 14
Malvinas, see Falkland Islands
Managua, 43, **44**
Mao Tse-tung, 22, 23
Marighela, Carlos, 33, 34, 49, 52
Maritime Exclusion Zone (MEZ), 39
Marti, Farabundo, 53
Maximillian, Archduke, 14
Mayorga, Silvio, 43
Menendez, Major-General Mario, 39, **39**, 40, 41

mestizos, 8, 9, 10
Mexican revolution, 11, **11**, 50
Mexico, 7, 8, 9, 23, 45, 47; revolution, 11, **11**, 21, 50; Texas, 13-14; and United States, 13-14, 15, 17, 27; Second World War, 17, debt crisis, 54, 55
Meza, General Garcia, 56
Minimanual of Urban Guerrilla Warfare, The, 33, 49
MIR (*Movimiento de Izquierdo Revolucionaria*), 30, 53
Mitrione, Dan, 35, 53
MLN (*Movimiento do Liberación Nacional*), see Tupamaros
Moncada Barracks, 23, 48
Monroe Doctrine, 14, 15, 17
Monroe, President James, 14
Montoneros, 36-37, 38, 42, 52, **52**
Montevideo, 16, 33-35
MR-13 (*Movimiento Revolucionario 13 de Noviembre*), 30, 53

Namphy, General Henri, 42
nationalisation, 19, 24, 27
National Guard (Nicaragua), 43-44, 46, 51
National Revolutionary Movement (MNR), 21
natural resources, 7, 11, 12, 27, 54, 55
Netherlands, 8, 17
Neves, Tancredo, 42
"New Cold War", 43
New Jewel Movement, 44, 47
Nicaragua, 10, 15, 21, 27, 29, 32, 35, 43-44, **43**, 45, 46, 47, **50**, 51, 52, 53

OAS, 17, 27, 31, 32, 39, 43
OBAN (*Operação Bandeirantes*), 34
Obregón, Alvaro, 11, 50
oil-producing countries, 54, 55
Organisation of American States, see OAS
Organisation of Eastern Caribbean States, 47
Ortega, Daniel, 44

País, Frank, 23-24
Panama, 7, 8, 14, 16, 44, 45, 47
Panama Canal, 7, 14-15, **15**, 22, 27, 44
Panama Canal Treaty, 44
Pan-Amazonian Highway, 54, **54**
Papa Doc, 20, 42, 49
Paraguay, 8, 9, 10, 13, **13**, 17, 29, 32, 35, 42, 43, 50
Pearl Harbor, 17
Pedro I, 9

Period of Africanization, 12
Perón, Colonel Juan Domingo, **18**, 19, **19**, 20, 36-37, 49, 52
Perón, Eva, **18**, 19, **19**, 49
Perón, Isabelita, 37, 49
Perónismo, 19, 36-37, **36, 37**
Peru, 7, 8, 9, 10, 12, 13, **13**, 17, 29, 42, 50, 53, 55, 56-57
petrodollars, 54, 55
Pinilla, Rojas, 21
Pinochet, Augusto, 35, 42, 49, **49**
Pizarro, Francisco, 7
Platt Amendment, 14
Plaza de Mayo, 38, **38**
Point Salines, 44, 47
Pombal, Marquis of, 8
Ponce, Juan Federico, 22
population, 7, 12, 33, 35
Portocarrero, Adolfo Calero, 46
Port San Carlos, 40, **41**
Port Stanley, 39, 40, **40, 41**, 51
Portugal, colonial empire, 7-8; independence, 8-10
propaganda, 27

Reagan, Ronald, 38, 45, 46-47
Reciprocal Trade Agreements Act, 15,
Rega, Lopez, 37
regionalists, 10, 12
Resolution 502, 39
Revolutionary Military Council, 47
Rio Treaty, 17, 39
Romero Mena, General Carlos Humberto, 45
Romero, Archbishop Oscar, 45
Roosevelt Corollary, 15, 17
Roosevelt, Franklin, 15
Roosevelt, Theodore, 15
Royal Marines, 39, 40

safe bases, 32, 34
Sandinista People's Army, 44
Sandinistas, 43-44, **43, 44**, 46, 47, 49, **50**, 51, 52, 53
Sandino, Augusto, 43
San Francisco Conference, 17
Sanguinetti, Julio, 42
San Martin, José de, 8, 9
San Martin, Ramon Grau, 48
Santa Anna, General Antonio López de, 13
Santa Cruz province, Bolivia, 30
Santo Domingo, 32, **32**
Sarney, José, 42
Sendero Luminoso, see Shining Path
Sendic, Raúl, 53
Sergeants' Revolt, 48
shanty towns, 33, 55, **55**
Shining Path, 42, 53
Somoza García, Anastasio, 21
Somoza (Junior), Anastasio, 21, 43, 46, 49, **49**, 51, 53

Somoza, Luis, 21, 49
South Georgia, 39, 51
Soviet Union, 22, 26-27, 28, 29, **29**, 31, 44-47, **50**
Spain, colonial empire, 7-8; independence, 8-10, 12; Cuba, 14
Stroessner, Alfredo, 42

Tegucigalpa, 43
Thatcher, Margaret, 38
Tierra del Fuego, 41
Tontons Macoutes, 20, 49
Torres, Camilo, 29
trade, **7**, 8, 9, 12, 15, 17, 18, 27
Tricontinental Conference, 29
Triple Alliance War, 12
Trotsky, Lev, 36
True Blue Medical School, 47
Trujillo Molina, Rafael Léonidas, 20, 32
Tupamaros, 34-35, 42, 53

Ubico, General Jorge, 22
United Fruit Company, 48
United Nations, 17, 54, 55
United Nations Security Council, 39
United States: Mexican Revolution, 11; Dominican Republic, 12, 32-33; and Mexico, 23-24; and Texas, 13-14; Monroe Doctrine and interventionism, 14-15, 16-17, 21; Cuba, 14, 22-25, **22, 25**, 26-28; Panama Canal, 14-15, 44; communism and Cold War, 17, 18, 22-25, 26-29, 31-32, 35, 44-47; armed forces, 27, 32, **32**, 46, 47; Chile, 35; Falklands War, 38, 39; Nicaragua, 44, 46; Grenada, 44, 47; debt crisis, 54, 55
United States Congress, 46
United States Marines, 32, 47
United States SEALs, 47
United States Special Forces ("Green Berets"), 31, 46
urban guerrillas, 33-35, 49
Urías, Colonel, Cesar Yánez, 20
Uruguay, 8, 12, 16-17, 18, 33-35, 36, 37, 42, 53, 55

Vargas, Getúlio, 20, **20**
Venezuela, 8, 10, 17, 20, 30, 47, 53, 54, 55
Videla, General Jorge, 37, 38
Villa, Pancho, 11, 50
Viola, General Roberto, 38
VPR (*Vanguarda Popular Revolucionaria*), 34

Wireless Ridge, 41
World Bank, 54, 55
World War, Second, 15-18, 26

Zapata, Emiliano, **10**, 11, 50

FURTHER READING

Blakemore, H, *Latin America* (Oxford University Press 1966)
Calvocoressi, P, *World Politics Since 1945* (Longman 1977)
Debray, R, *Che's Guerrilla War* (Penguin Books 1975)
Diedrich, B and Burt, A, *Papa Doc* (Penguin Books 1969)
Dorschner, J and Fabricio, R, *The Winds of December. The Cuban Revolution 1958* (Macmillan 1980)
Dunkerley, J, *The Long War. Dictatorship and Revolution in El Salvador* (Junction Books 1982)
English, A, *Armed Forces of Latin America* (Jane's 1984)
Fagg, J E, *Latin America. A General History* (Macmillan New York 3rd edn 1977)
Gott, R, *Guerrilla Movements in Latin America* (Thomas Nelson 1970)
Gott, R, *Guide to the Political Parties of South America* (Penguin Books 1973)
Guevara, E ("Che"), *Reminiscences of the Cuban Revolutionary War* (Monthly Review Press, New York 1968)
Guevara, E ("Che"), *Guerrilla Warfare* (Penguin Books 1972)
Gunther, J, *Inside South America* (Hamish Hamilton 1967)
Hastings, M and Jenkins, S, *The Battle for the Falklands* (Michael Joseph 1983)

International Institute for Strategic Studies: "Military Balance" and "Strategic Survey" (annual publications)
Keegan, J (ed), *World Armies* (Macmillan 2nd edn 1983)
Marighela, C, *For the Liberation of Brazil* (Penguin Books 1971)
Niedergang, M, *The Twenty Latin Americas* (2 vols Penguin Books 1971)
O'Shaughnessy, H, *Grenada. Revolution, Invasion and Aftermath* (Sphere Books 1984)
Pearce, J, *Under the Eagle. US Intervention in Central America and the Caribbean* (Latin American Bureau 1982)
Pendle, G, *A History of Latin America* (Penguin Books 1975)
Summerlin, S, *Latin America. The Land of Revolution* (Franklin Watts, New York 1972)
Thomas, H, *Cuba or the Pursuit of Freedom* (Eyre and Spottiswoode 1971)
War in Peace Partwork (Orbis 1983-85)
Wyden, P, *Bay of Pigs. The Untold Story* (Jonathan Cape 1979)

(Note: All publishers located in London unless specified otherwise)

ACKNOWLEDGEMENTS

Page 5: Susan Meiselas/John Hillelson Agency; page 7: Keystone/Photosource; page 8: BBC Hulton Picture Library; page 10: BBC Hulton; page 11: Mary Evans Library; page 15: Stern; page 16: Keystone/Photosource; page 18: Popperfoto; page 19: Rex Features; page 20: Keystone/Photosource; page 21: Popperfoto; page 23: BBC Hulton; page 25: Popperfoto; page 28: Keystone/Photosource; page 29: Topham; page 31: Keystone/Photosource; page 32-33: Keystone/Photosource; page 34: Stern; page 35: Rex Features; page 36: Rex Features; page 37: Keystone/Photosource; page 38: Rex Features; page 39: Frank Spooner Agency; page 40: Frank Spooner Agency; page 42: Topham; page 43: John Hillelson Agency; page 44: Stern; page 45: Rex Features; page 48(all): Popperfoto; page 49(all): Popperfoto; page 50: Popperfoto; page 51: Frank Spooner Agency; page 52: Popperfoto; page 53: Popperfoto; page 54: Frank Spooner Agency; page 55: Hutchison Library; page 56: Frank Spooner Agency; page 57: Frank Spooner Agency.